Shoreline Quilts

COMPILED BY CYNDY LYLE RYMER

C&T PUBLISHING

©2003 C&T Publishing
Editor-in-Chief: Darra Williamson
Editor: Cyndy Lyle Rymer
Technical Editors: Karyn Hoyt-Culp, Franki Kohler
Copyeditor/Proofreader: Mary Elizabeth Johnson/Stacy Chamness
Cover Designer: Aliza Shalit
Back Cover Designer: Kirstie L. McCormick
Book Designer: Dawn DeVries Sokol
Design Director: Diane Pedersen
Illustrator: Kate Reed
Production Assistant: Kirstie L. McCormick
Photography: Sharon Risedorph, Cyndy Lyle Rymer
Published by C&T Publishing, Inc., P.O. Box 1456, Lafayette,
California 94549
Front cover: *Adicora* by Babette Grunwald (page 10), photo by
Sharon Risedorph
Back cover: *Pauli's Ocean View* by Mickey Depre (page 64), photo by
Sharon Risedorph

Attention Copy Shops: Please note the following exception—Publisher
and contributors give permission to photocopy pages 13, 20, 28, 34, 41,
42, 47, 50, 55, 59, 63, 67, 73, 78, 79, 80, 81, 85, 86, 87, and 88 for
personal use only.

Attention Teachers: C&T Publishing, Inc. encourages you to use
this book as a text for teaching. Contact us at 800-284-1114 or
www.ctpub.com for more information about the C&T Teachers Program.

We take great care to ensure that the information included in this book
is accurate and presented in good faith, but no warranty is provided nor
results guaranteed. Having no control over the choices of materials or
procedures used, neither the author nor C&T Publishing, Inc. shall have
any liability to any person or entity with respect to any loss or damage
caused directly or indirectly by the information contained in this book.
For your convenience, we post an up-to-date listing of corrections on
our web page (www.ctpub.com). If a correction is not already noted,
please contact our customer service department at ctinfo@ctpub.com or
at P.O. Box 1456, Lafayette, CA 94549.

Trademarked (™) and Registered Trademark (®) names are used
throughout this book. Rather than use the symbols with every occur-
rence of a trademark and registered trademark name, we are using the
names only in the editorial fashion and to the benefit of the owner, with
no intention of infringement.

Library of Congress Cataloging-in-Publication Data

Shoreline quilts : 15 glorious get-away projects / compiled by Cyndy
Lyle Rymer.
    p. cm.
Includes bibliographical references and index.
  ISBN 1-57120-201-3 (paper trade)
  1. Patchwork--Patterns. 2. Quilting. 3. Patchwork quilts. 4.
Seashore in art. 5. Beaches in art. I. Rymer, Cyndy Lyle. II.
Title.
  TT835 .S473 2003
  746.46'041--dc21
                              2002015013

Printed in China
10 9 8 7 6 5 4 3 2 1

In loving memory of my grandmother, Margaret Brown, who
first introduced me to the pleasures of the New Jersey shore;
to my mother, Marie Lyle, for continuing the tradition on
the West coast; to my family, John, Kev, Zack, Zana, and
Arlo, with whom I have shared incredible moments on
many beaches; and to Karyn Hoyt-Culp and Timothy Culp,
who have had to surf some rough waters during the production of this book.

Thanks to all of the people who made *Shoreline Quilts* possible,
especially the contributing artists. This book would not have
been possible without the help and shared enthusiasm of Anna
Poor, David and Peter Mancuso, Mary Carlson of Tumbleweed
Quilts in West Barnstable, Massachusetts, and all of the terrific
people at C&T.

The Road to the Beach
6 1/2" x 8 1/4", Lucy Grijalva, Benicia, California. Based
on block patterns from *The Foundation Piecer*.

Table of Contents

Sandcastles and Seashells

50" x 41½", Carol Lohrenz, Eagle, ID, 2001
Machine pieced and photo transfer.

My granddaughter and I have a special beach where we have played "make believe" since she could barely walk. I created this memory quilt for her. My sisters and I planned a quilting retreat on the Oregon Coast, and I created this design as a mystery block-of-the-month quilt to be our retreat memory quilt. This quilt holds double memories for me: playing on the beach with my granddaughter, and sewing by the sea with my sisters.

This book allows a glimpse into the love affair that most of us land-dwellers have with the sea. The contributing artists were all drawn to represent the same subject for countless reasons. Some of these quilts are reminders of time spent at the water's edge. They are snap-shots of happy memories; others show gangs of undersea creatures. We are fascinated by these living things that look, move, and even breathe so differently from ourselves. Some look with reverence and even fear at the power that these beautiful waters can unleash when fueled by storms on the open ocean.

These quilts were made across the country by artists living in both coastal areas and landlocked ones. They depict scenes viewed by the makers from their windows, in postcards, in their imaginations, in memories from vacations taken long ago, or through the lens of a diving mask.

A number of these works of art were displayed in an exhibition curated by Mancuso Show Management, entirely of sea-themed quilts. Visitors to the Quilt & Sewing Fest at Myrtle Beach in the spring of 2002 were the first to view this ocean-inspired collection.

Enjoy finding your own inspiration in the pages of this book. Whatever draws you to the sea, have fun representing it in your own shoreline quilt!

Anna L. Poor, Mancuso Show Management

Sea of Dreams

51" x 58", Susan Brittingham, Riner, VA, 2000
Machine pieced, appliquéd, trapunto, and quilted; embellished with a variety of beads.

A voyage on the *Sea of Dreams* can be taken on many levels, from simple to profound.
This composition invites its viewers to embark on a journey to another land, another
time, another reality. Although I have used columns in my work previously, my goal here
was to maximize the illusion of roundness and depth.

Down by the Sea

This book existed in my "sea of dreams" for quite a long time. A serendipitous email announcing the first-ever "Down by the Sea" quilt festival sponsored by the Mancusos was the catalyst for making the dream book a reality. With help from David and Peter Mancuso and Anna Poor, and the willing enthusiasm of the quiltmakers whose work is showcased here, we launched *Shoreline Quilts*.

Memories of time spent near an ocean, lake, or river have an incredible ability to soothe the soul. Like many

people, when I need solace or rejuvenation I head to a beach for a long walk and to watch the waves. Any body of water has a mesmerizing effect: the calmness of a still lake or bay is so soothing, while the crashing of powerful waves against the rocks is enervating. I am happiest when I'm *in* the water; I like to fantasize that I was a mermaid in a previous life.

Who doesn't feel inspired by the intensity of color in the brilliant turquoise of tropical waters, the deeper blues and greens of northern oceans, or even the muddy browns of a river swollen with snow melt? The incredible range of colors and moods associated with water is so awe-inspiring, yet so difficult for some of us to capture with fabric.

But the quiltmakers featured here have found many successful ways to interpret their visions using all of the tricks and techniques that quilters have at their disposal. All it takes is patience, perseverance, and a healthy dose of risk-taking.

Traditional quilters will enjoy tackling quilts like *Pleiades Pineapple* on page 30 with it's stunning use of the Pineapple block, *Stars at Sea* on page 70 with the foundation-pieced Storm at Sea blocks, or *A Day at the Beach* with the ingenious use of a variety of Log Cabin blocks. *Tsunami Morning: Wave of Grief*, page 22, has its

roots in traditional quiltmaking with its base of Lady of the Lake blocks, but is embellished with painted cheesecloth and organza. *Pauli's Ocean View*, page 64, features a similar block, but goes way beyond the traditional with its stunning use of appliqué and ornamentation, such as the secret message-in-a-bottle with its own tiny cork.

Quilters who want to give reverse appliqué a try will enjoy making *Kissing Dolphins* or *Cape Cod Lobsters* on pages 56 and 60. The three delightful, smaller quilts on pages 44–52 evolved from a Block-of-the-Month series at Tumbleweed Quilts in West Barnstable, Massachusetts, and can be either hand or machine appliquéd.

Traditional quilters may also enjoy the challenge of giving the more improvisational techniques a try. The cover quilt, *Adicora*, on page 10, was put together collage-style, and includes great use of embellishment. *Goldenrod on the Beach* (page 90) was constructed in a similar, quilt-as-you-sew manner, and offers opportunities for hand embroidered decoration.

For lighthouse lovers, *Fundy* (page 76) represents a fun challenge with its combination of more traditional Snail's Trail blocks and freezer-paper pieced lighthouse blocks. This quilt could easily be adapted to include the lighthouses that have special meaning to you.

There are many other incredible quilts throughout the book that will inspire you to dig into your stash to create your own treasures. All it takes is a little dreaming, and a willingness to spend the time translating your visions with fabric and thread. Put on some calypso music or ocean sounds, dance a little, and have fun!

Cyndy Lyle Rymer
Editor and part-time mermaid

A Return to Lila's Garden

51" x 75", Cyndy Lyle Rymer, Danville, CA, 1990
Machine pieced and quilted, dimensional appliqué.

When a friend from Vermont sent me a postcard of an oil painting by the late Eleanor Daniels, I knew I had to make a quilt. I spent two wonderful summers at a camp on the Vermont side of Lake Champlain. I began the quilt in a class called "Radiant Nine-Patch" taught by Carol Wight Jones, and worked like a woman possessed making nine-patches, ruched flowers, and paper-pieced sailboats and leaves while my two young boys played nearby. I have many happy memories of camp, and of making the quilt. It is still my favorite. Many thanks to Sherwood A. Davies for permission to interpret Eleanor's painting.

Happiness Is Swimming with a Few Friends

(left to right) 36" x 103", 36" x 78", 36" x 103"
Lynne L. Gettelfinger, Rock Hill, SC, 2001–2002
Raw-edge appliqué and free-motion embroidery with machine bobbin work and quilting.

I have always been fascinated by the beauty, color, movement, and wonder of ocean wildlife. For years I collected books and photos of underwater scenes, coral reefs, and fish. Studying several books, including Susan Carlson's *Free-Style Quilts*, helped me to see how to achieve the effect of depth and perspective with fabric. *Happiness Is Swimming with a Few Friends* was my first actual ocean theme quilt. I finished the first (left) panel in April 2001 to hang in time for viewing by the guests who arrived for my son's wedding. Without another deadline as a motivator, I did not finish the last two panels until 2002. Gaining some acceptance and approval for my first quilt has served to really motivate me to create more; this is what I love to do!

adicora

Babette Grunwald, Prosser, WA, 2002
Finished quilt size: 42" x 21"

This easy collage-style quilt was inspired by the colors and fun I experienced in Adicora, a small fisherman's village on the Paraguana Peninsula of Venezuela. Our days were filled with walks on the beach hunting for shells, surfing the waves, and flying kites in the strong winds. Our tired bodies were soothed by tropical dinners and the gentle rocking of the hammocks at night.

FABRIC REQUIREMENTS

Muslin (or similar fabric): ⅔ yard for foundation

Light blues, light grays, and violets: ⅛ yard each of 5 fabrics for the sky

Dark blues: ⅛ yard each of 5 fabrics for the ocean

Light yellows and beiges: ⅛ yard each of 5 fabrics for the beach

Brights: assorted scraps (approximately 5" x 5") for the cabins, kites, and sailboats

Brown: 2 scraps (approximately 5" x 5") for the tree trunks

Green: 5 scraps (approximately 5" x 5") for the leaves

Burgundy tulle: ⅔ yard

Backing: ¾ yard

Batting: 46" x 25"

Binding: ⅓ yard

Other supplies

Cardboard: approximately 46" x 25"

Chalk

Buttons, ribbons (for the kite tail), beads, and other charms and "beachy" objects

Basting adhesive spray

CUTTING

Foundation muslin: Cut a rectangle 42" x 21".

Dark blues, light blues, light grays, violets, light yellows, beiges: Cut 1½" to 2"-wide strips, then cut strips into 4" to 5" rectangles.

Brights, greens, and brown: Cut cabins, cabin inserts, doors, windows, roofs, roof inserts, palm trunks, palm leaves, kites, and sailboats freehand or use the templates on page 13.

Binding: Cut 4 strips 2½" wide.

QUILT TOP ASSEMBLY

The background is assembled collage-style on top of the muslin or similar fabric. You can use a glue stick —lightly—to hold scraps in place until you add the layer of tulle (page 12).

Background layer

1 Lay the foundation fabric on the large piece of cardboard.

2 Divide the foundation fabric into 3 approximately equal horizontal parts for the sky, ocean, and the beach. Mark divisions with chalk lines.

Divide muslin into 3 sections.

3 Lay the sky fabrics over the top third of your base fabric, overlapping the rectangles by ¼". Avoid placing the same fabrics beside one another. Completely cover the top third; no foundation fabric should show.

4 Lay the ocean fabrics over the middle third of the foundation.

5 Cover the bottom third with beach fabrics.

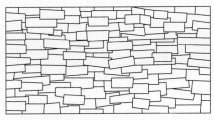

Completed background

Cabins, trees, and sailboats

1 Arrange the 5 cabins on the beach area, allowing space for the 3 palm trees. Place house inserts, windows, doors, roofs, and roof inserts on top of the cabins. (Note that the peaks of the roofs overlap the beach/water line.)

2 Position the palm tree trunks, palm leaves, and sailboats.

3 Step back from your design and make any changes. (You may want to take a break at this point.)

4 Use a dry iron to press your work on the cardboard, being careful not to move your work around. All the pieces need to be completely flat.

Foreground shapes composed

Tulle placement

The purpose of the tulle is to anchor all the design pieces in place until they are secured by quilting. Once the quilting is finished, the tulle is hardly noticeable.

1 Work on half the design at a time. Spray lightly with basting spray, and smooth the tulle over the sprayed area, making sure all the fabric pieces are flat.

2 Keep the loose tulle folded back, and spray the second half of your quilt. Smooth the tulle flat. Your piece should now be entirely covered with tulle, and all your design pieces should be secured in place.

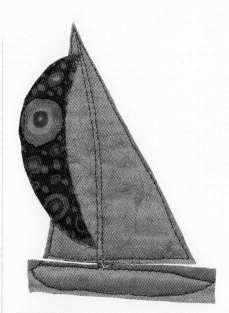

Finishing

See Quilting Basics, page 93, for general quilting and finishing instructions.

1 Layer the backing, batting, and quilt top/foundation. Pin, thread, or spray-baste.

2 Quilt with free-motion quilting using any preferred design, or follow one of the quilting suggestions.

3 Trim the excess batting and backing with a rotary cutter, squaring the quilt as you trim.

4 Bind.

Embellishments

1 Make a kite by placing 2 small pieces of fabric right sides together and cutting a diamond shape. Stitch a ¼" seam around the edge, leaving 1" open.

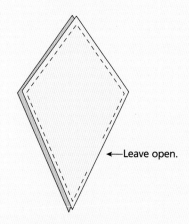

←Leave open.

Stitch around kite edges.

2 Turn right side out. Stitch opening closed and appliqué in place on top of the tulle.

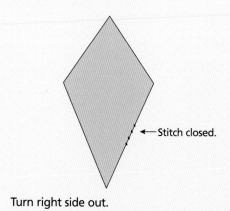

←Stitch closed.

Turn right side out.

3 Embellish with buttons, ribbons, and small charms and other beachy objects.

4 Add a hanging sleeve and label.

Quilting suggestions

Enlarge these patterns 260%, or create your own.

Connie Carrington, Huntsville, AL, 2001
Finished quilt size: 56" x 67"

The Spiral block design is an original design by Christiane Meunier and appeared in her book Easy Art Quilts, *published by Chitra Publications, 2000.*

Just below the water's surface, quiet, swaying currents are a sanctuary from the chaotic man-made world above. Diagonal strips of color form sonar waves that traverse the sea, and green sea plants sway in the currents. Inspired by the thread paintings of Libby Lehman and Ellen Ann Eddy, metallic fish swim in the warm waters, surrounded by bead bubbles.

FABRIC REQUIREMENTS

Medium and dark turquoises: assorted to total ¼ yard for sonar strips in borders

Blues and turquoises: assorted to total 3⅝ yards for sonar blocks and background triangles

Yellows: assorted to total ¼ yard for sonar strips

Oranges: assorted to total ¼ yard for sonar strips

Dark oranges: assorted to total ¼ yard for sonar strips

Lime greens: assorted to total ⅛ yard for seagrass strips

Medium blue: ½ yard for narrow inner borders

Dark blue: ½ yard for wide outer borders

Backing: 3½ yards

Batting: 60" x 71"

Binding: ½ yard

Other supplies

Iron-on tear-away stabilizer

Assorted colors of thick and thin metallic, rayon, or neon threads for thread-painted fish

Colored yarns for couched corals

Clear invisible thread for couching and machine appliqué

Green silk ribbon for hand embroidery of seaweeds (optional)

Assorted round beads for bubbles and scales on small fish

Assorted long, flat beads for schools of small fish

CUTTING

Medium and dark turquoises: Cut 5 strips 1¾" x 8½" and 7 strips 1¾" x 5½".

Blues and turquoises: Cut 42 squares 7" x 7".

Cut 39 squares 6½" x 6½", then cut in half diagonally for large background triangles.

Cut 18 squares 4¾" x 4¾", then cut in half diagonally for small background triangles.

Yellows: Cut 10 strips 1¾" x 9½" for sonar strips.

Oranges: Cut 8 strips 1¾" x 9½" for sonar strips.

Dark oranges: Cut 6 strips 1¾" x 9½" for sonar strips.

Lime greens: Cut 13 strips 1" x 9½" and 3 strips 1" x 4½".

Medium blues: Cut 6 strips 2½" x width of the fabric. Seam together as needed to cut:

2 strips 2½" x 48½" for the top and bottom borders

1 strip 2½" x 63½" for the left side border

1 strip 2½" x 33½" for the middle of the right side border

5 strips 2½" x 6" for the top and bottom of the right side border

Dark blue: Cut 3 strips 4½" x width of the fabric. Seam together as needed to cut:

1 strip 4½" x 52½" for the bottom border

1 strip 4½" x 71" for the right border

Binding: Cut 7 strips 2" x width of fabric for binding.

BLOCK ASSEMBLY

Sonar blocks

Finished size: 5½"

1 On the *wrong* side of 21 of the 7" x 7" squares, draw diagonal lines from corner to corner in both directions. With right sides together, pair a marked square with an unmarked square. Sew ¼" away from the marked line on both sides of one diagonal. Make 21 units.

2 Cut each square in quarters on the two drawn lines to make 84 **quarter-square triangles**. Open and press the seam allowances to one side. You have completed half of the Sonar block.

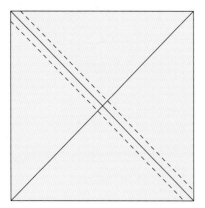

Sew on dashed lines, cut on solid lines.

3 For the other half of the block, select 24 small background triangles and the 24 sonar strips. Fold each sonar strip in half, and finger-press the fold to mark the center. Fold each triangle in half and finger-press to mark the center of its long side. With right sides together, align the center of the strip with the center of the triangle, and sew with a ¼" seam. Press seam allowances toward the strip.

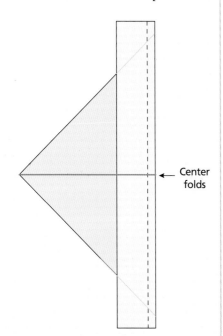

Align center folds and sew.

4 Center and sew a pieced quarter-square triangle to the opposite side of the sonar strip, aligning the seam with the center fold mark on the strip. Press seam allowances toward the strip.

5 Trim each sonar block to a 6" x 6" square, making sure the seamlines end precisely at the corners of the block.

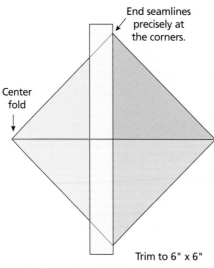

End seamlines precisely at the corners.

Center fold

Trim to 6" x 6"

Sonar block

Background blocks
Finished size: 5½", 5³⁄₁₆"

1 For the 45 background blocks, fold a large background triangle in half and finger-press to mark its long side. Center and sew to a pieced quarter-square triangle. Press seams toward the background triangle.

2 Trim 40 background blocks to 6" x 6" squares, making sure the seamlines end precisely at the corners. Trim the remaining 5 background blocks to 5¹¹⁄₁₆" x 5¹¹⁄₁₆" square, making sure the seamlines end at the corners.

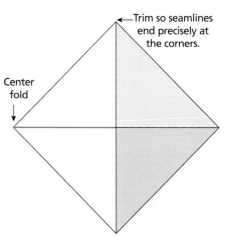

Trim so seamlines end precisely at the corners.

Center fold

Background block

Seagrass blocks
Finished size: 5¹¹⁄₁₆"

1 Select 13 large background triangles to use in the seagrass blocks. Fold each triangle in half and finger-press to mark the center of its long side. Fold each 1" x 9½" lime green strip in half and finger-press. Align the center of the strip with the center of the triangle, and sew the strip to the triangle along its long side.

2 Center and sew a pieced quarter-square triangle to the opposite side of the green strip, aligning the seam with the fold mark on the strip. Press seam toward the strip.

3 Trim each seagrass block to a 5¹¹⁄₁₆" x 5¹¹⁄₁₆" square, making sure that the seamlines end precisely at the corners of the block.

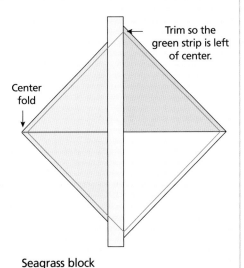

Trim so the green strip is left of center.

Center fold

Seagrass block

Seagrass border triangles

1 For the 3 seagrass border triangles, sew a 1" x 4½" lime green strip to a small background triangle. Press seam allowances toward the strip.

2 Sew another small background triangle to the other side of the strip, and press seam allowances toward the center. Trim the triangle to 5¹¹⁄₁₆" by laying it on top of a seagrass block and allowing a ¼" seam allowance along the block diagonal. Make sure the green strip lies to the left of the center diagonal line.

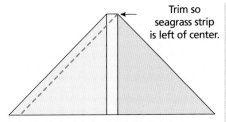

Trim so seagrass strip is left of center.

Seagrass border triangle

QUILT TOP ASSEMBLY

It is easiest to assemble the pieced center of the quilt top in quarter sections because the seagrass section is on point, and the other three sections are in straight rows. Begin with the seagrass quarter section at the lower left, then work counterclockwise around the quilt top.

Lower-left section

1 Arrange the 13 seagrass blocks on point, using the 5 background blocks that are 5¹¹⁄₁₆" square to fill in as shown.

2 Place the 3 seagrass border triangles along the bottom, and use 9 large background triangles to fill in to make a square. Add 2 small background triangles; one in the upper-left corner and one in the lower-right corner.

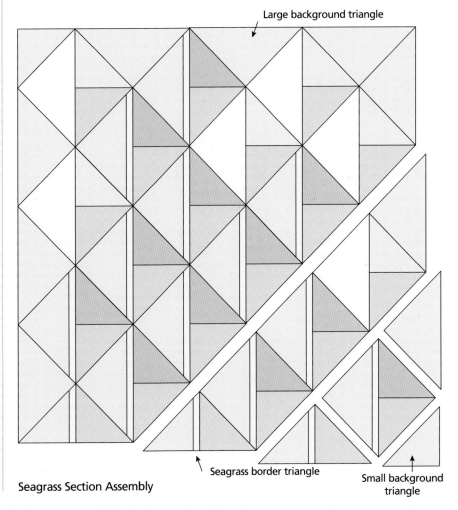

Large background triangle

Seagrass border triangle

Small background triangle

Seagrass Section Assembly

3 Sew the seagrass blocks into diagonal rows. Press the seams in each row in alternate directions so they nest when you sew the rows together. Sew the rows into a square. Press seams in one direction. The background triangles will be slightly larger than needed, so trim them even with the edges of the seagrass blocks.

Lower-right section

1 To make the lower-right quarter section you will need 9 sonar blocks and 7 background blocks. Arrange them in 4 rows of 4 blocks, referring to the Quilt Assembly Diagram for placement. (Note that the small pieced background triangles point to the lower-left corner.) Sew the blocks together into rows. Press the seams in each row in alternate directions so they nest together when you sew the rows together. Sew the rows together to make a square. Press the seams in one direction.

2 A short strip of triangles is added to the bottom edge. Sew together 4 large background triangles and a pieced half-square triangle; add small background triangles to either end. This border will be slightly longer than needed and will need to be trimmed after it is sewn in place. Sew the strip of triangles to the bottom edge.

3 Sew the lower-right quarter section to the lower-left seagrass section to make the bottom half of the quilt. Press the seam to one side.

Top section

1 Arrange 33 pieced 6" background blocks and 15 sonar blocks into 6 rows of 8 blocks for the top of the quilt, as shown in the Quilt Assembly Diagram.
Note that the small pieced background triangles point to the *upper* left in the top half of the quilt, to the *lower*-left corner in the bottom row.

2 Sew the blocks into 6 rows of 8 blocks, then sew the rows into a rectangle.

3 A short strip of triangles is added to the left edge of the top section. Sew together 8 large background triangles. Add small background triangles to either end. This

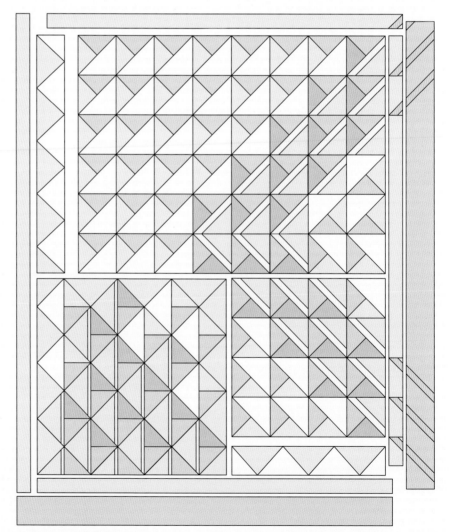

Quilt Assembly Diagram

border will be slightly longer than needed and will need to be trimmed after it is sewn in place. Sew the strip of triangles to the left side.

4 Sew the top and bottom halves of the quilt together. Press the seam to one side.

Inner border assembly

1 To add the sonar wave to the top right corner of the border, draw a 45° diagonal line from the outside corner of the upper border strip. Mark a line ¼" inside this sewing line and cut. Save the small triangle that is cut away.

Cut the top border at a 45° angle.

2 Sew a 5½" x 1¾"-wide strip of medium turquoise on the diagonal sewing line; press the seam allowances away from the strip. Align the saved triangle on the other side of the turquoise strip so the bottom edge of the triangle will be even with the bottom edge of the border strip. Sew in place. Trim the border strip so the diagonal sewing line will go in the corner.

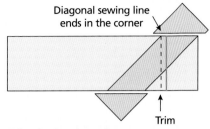

Diagonal sewing line ends in the corner

Trim

Trim the border strip.

3 For the narrow right side border segments, sew the sonar waves to the 2" x 6" strips. Follow the same process as for the top border corner described in Steps 1 and 2. For the top 2 segments, sew the sonar waves to the bottom of the strips. For the 3 bottom segments, sew the sonar waves to the top of the strips.

4 Sew the top two sonar wave segments to the 2½" x 33½" right side border strip, then add the bottom three sonar wave segments.

5 Sew this right inner border to the right side of the quilt, matching seams on the sonar blocks.

6 Sew the top border to the quilt top, placing the sonar wave segment on the right side, matching seams. Add the bottom inner border. Add the left side border last.

7 Trim the borders to square the quilt.

Outer border assembly

The dark blue outer border is added to the bottom and right side of the quilt; the sonar waves are pieced into the right outer border.

1 As with the inner border, starting at the top of the 4½" x 71"

right outer border strip, draw a diagonal sewing line starting 2½" below the left corner and running upward at a 45° angle to the outside edge. Cut a ¼" seam allowance outside of this sewing line. Sew a 1¾" strip of medium turquoise fabric along this diagonal seamline. Press the seam upward.

2 Align a ruler so the ¼" seam allowance on the inner edge of the border is covered and the long edge of the ruler is along the seamline. Measure down from the bottom of the triangle at the corner 3¾" along the seamline, and place a mark at that spot, on the inner border seamline. Draw a 45° sewing line up through this mark.

3 Cut a ¼" seam allowance below this sewing line, and sew a medium turquoise sonar strip along this seamline. Press the seam upward.

4 Repeat the process in Step 2, marking on the ¼" seam allowance at a point 3¾" down from the last sonar strip. Add the last upper sonar strip. Press the seam upward.

5 Again align a ruler so the ¼" inner seam allowance is cov-

Enlarge 200%.

Enlarge 200%.

ered, measure down and mark 33½" from the lowest sonar strip seamline. Draw a downward diagonal seamline on the border fabric, and cut a ¼" seam allowance below this

line. Sew a dark turquoise strip along this diagonal line. Press.

6 Add two more sonar strips, measuring down 3¾" from the

last sonar seamline. Trim the sonar strips so the border is 4½" wide.

7 Sew the lower dark blue border to the quilt, then the right side border, matching seams at the sonar strips. Trim the border lengths to square the quilt.

THREAD-PAINTED FISH

1 Enlarge and trace the fish shapes, or draw your own fish, on the paper side of tear-away stabilizer. Be sure to include details such as eyes, fins, and regions of different colors. Allow at least 1" of stabilizer around each fish. Do not cut out the fish shape. Iron the stabilizer in place on the back of the quilt top. **Note that the fish motif will be reversed on the quilt front.**

2 With the stabilizer side up so you can see your lines, stitch along the outline of the fish, using an appropriate thread color in the **bobbin**. This will mark your fish outline on the quilt front.

3 Lightly fill in the fish outline with free-motion stitching, using metallic, rayon, or neon threads. Try a circular motion

stitch for fish scales, and parallel lines on fins and tails. Stitching can be done from either the front or the back. If you are using heavier metallic or other decorative threads, wind the thread on the bobbin, and stitch from the back using the lines that were drawn on the stabilizer.

4 After the free-motion stitching on each fish is complete, tear off the stabilizer around the outside of the motif. Leave the stabilizer under the thread-painted areas. Lightly press the fish, using a medium-hot iron on the quilt back.

5 To create corals on the sea floor, sketch the coral shape on the paper side of the tear-away stabilizer. Iron it to the back of the quilt where the inner and outer borders meet. Stitch around the coral shape, using an appropriate thread color in the bobbin. On the quilt front, couch decorative yarns in a meandering shape to simulate coral using invisible thread. Leave enough length on the yarn ends to bring them to the quilt back with a crewel needle. Tear away the stabilizer around the coral after couching is complete.

FINISHING

See Quilting Basics, page 93, for general quilting and finishing instructions.

1 Layer the quilt top, batting, and backing. Spray or pin-baste for machine quilting.

2 Quilt around the fish motifs and the coral. Quilt small schools of fish swimming around the big fish, and starfish and crabs on the sea floor. Use meandering circular stitches to simulate pebbles on the bottom.

3 Bind.

4 If desired, add silk ribbon embroidery seaweed growing from the ocean floor. Add beads to simulate strings of bubbles trailing back from the fish. Sew beads on the sides of the small quilted fish, and add long flat beads to mimic schools of fish.

5 Add a hanging sleeve and label your quilt.

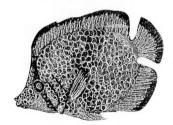

tsunami morning
wave of grief

Beth Stewart-Ozark, Lexington, SC, 1999
Finished quilt size: 51½" x 63½"

The creative process touched me profoundly when my godmother died unexpectedly. She knew I had been struggling to design a quilt using the Storm at Sea block. With her passing, I felt a huge wave of grief that led me to Tsunami Morning: Wave of Grief.

The red sky in this quilt represents hearing of her death in the wee hours of the morning. (I was in the Navy some years ago, so "Red sky at morning, sailor take warning" fits here as well.) In each Storm at Sea block there is a bright blue center; this represents her legacy of unconditional love to me. She would have loved the bright colors in this quilt, and making it helped me to recover from her absence, which came far too soon.

FABRIC REQUIREMENTS

Storm at Sea blocks

Red, red-orange, orange, yellow-orange, and yellow: 3 or 4 assorted fat quarters (18" x 22") of each color

Purple, lavender, pinkish-red, red-violet: 3 or 4 assorted fat quarters of each color

Green, green-gold, aqua, turquoise, blue-green: 4 to 6 assorted fat quarters of each color

Bright blue: ⅝ yard solid for the block centers

Blue-green: ½ yard for inner border strips

Lady of the Lake border blocks

Light blue, blue-silver, blue-gray, gray, and white: 8 assorted fat quarters

Dark blues: 8 assorted fat quarters

Organza: Lavender and pale purple (a variety of shades gives a better effect): 2 fat quarters of each for clouds

Backing: 3½ yards

Batting: 55" x 67"

Binding: ½ yard

Other supplies

Flannel or vinyl flannel-backed table-cloth for design wall

Template plastic (or sets A and C of Marti Michell's 3" Perfect Patchwork Templates; see Resources, page 96) for Storm at Sea blocks

Fusible web: One yard

One package of white cheesecloth for ocean foam

Fabric paints: silver, emerald, cobalt and turquoise for cheesecloth (Setacolor Sun Paints are recommended. See Resources, page 96.)

Aluminum oven-liner tray for painting cheesecloth

4 pint containers for mixing paint

4 foam brushes

Fabric spray adhesive

Masking tape and newsprint

Clear invisible thread

Cotton, rayon, and metallic thread to match ocean and sky

Optional bobbin work: Iridescent white metallic yarn (YLI Candlelight RNBO and an extra bobbin case for bobbin work are recommended.)

Darning or chenille needle

CUTTING

Storm at Sea blocks

Trace and cut the patterns on page 28 from template plastic (or use "Perfect Patchwork Templates").

Bright blue fabric: Cut one strip 3" wide, then crosscut into 12 squares 3" x 3" for the centers.

Blue-green: Cut the following strips on the lengthwise grain of the fabric for the inner borders: 2 strips 2" x 51½", 2 strips 2" x 48½", and 4 strips 2" x 6½" for the inner borders.

Each Storm at Sea block is unique. Study the photo and cut block patches individually to make sure your colors will produce the wave and sky. The number to cut of each patch is printed on the patterns on page 28. Audition fabrics to achieve the curve of the wave.

Border blocks

1 Pair each of the 8 dark blue fat quarters, right sides together, with one of the 8 light blue, gray, or white fat quarters.

2 From each pair, cut a 5⅜" strip; cut the strip into 2 squares 5⅜" x 5⅜", then cut each square diagonally. Repeat to make 64 large triangles. Keep the pairs together as they are cut so they will be in position for chain piecing. Label each pair of large triangles.

3 From the fabric remaining from the pairs of fat quarters, cut 2 strips 2⅜" long, then cut 14 squares 2⅜" x 2⅜". Cut each square on the diagonal to make a total of 448 small triangles. Keep small triangles together as they are cut to facilitate chain piecing.
Cheesecloth: Cut the cheesecloth into one-yard sections.
Binding: Cut 6 strips 2" wide.

BLOCK ASSEMBLY

Storm at Sea blocks

Finished size: 12" x 12"

Place the 12 bright blue center squares on your design wall in 4 rows of 3, leaving plenty of space around each square to place the remaining pattern pieces for each block. Work

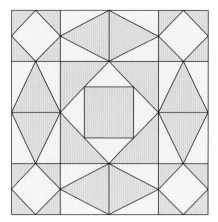

Storm at Sea block

on one block at a time so you can keep track of color placement.

1 Make the center section for each block first. Sew B triangles to either side of the center squares. Press seam allowances toward the center.

2 Sew B triangles to the top and bottom of the center squares; press seam allowances away from the center.

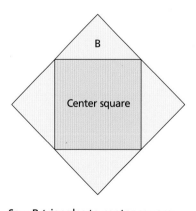

Sew B triangles to center square.

3 As in Step 2, add C triangles to this square-within-a-square. Press the side seam allowances toward the center, and the top and bottom away from the center to reduce bulk.

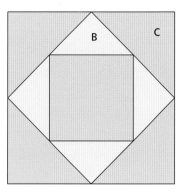

Add C triangles.

4 Sew 4 G triangles to each F square as in Steps 1 and 2. Make 4. (These are the corners of the Storm at Sea block.)

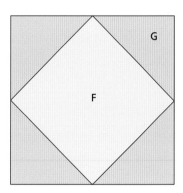

Make 4 Storm at Sea corners.

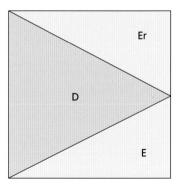

Make 8 per block.

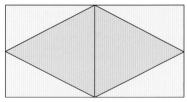

Make 4 pairs per block.

5 Sew an E and an E reverse (Er) to a D triangle. Make 8. Sew the E/D/Er squares in pairs.

6 For each block, arrange the completed block sections and sew them into 3 strips.
   Tip: Make sure you pin the matching points together so they meet at the seamline.

7 Sew the 3 strips together to finish each block. Again, pin to match points. Make 12 blocks.

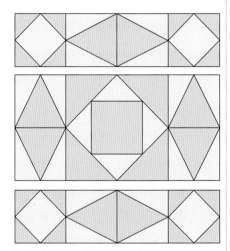

Sew the 3 sections together.

Lady of the Lake border blocks
Finished size: 6" x 6"

1 The 64 large triangles make 32 large half-square triangle units; 448 small triangles make the 224 small half-square triangle units. Chain-piece all of the large and small triangle pairs. Press seams open.

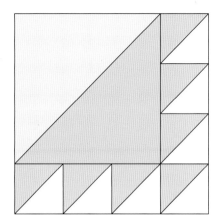

Lady of the Lake block

2 Chain-piece 32 sets of 3 small half-square triangle units.

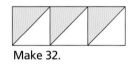

Make 32.

3 Chain-piece 32 sets of 4 small half-square triangle units.

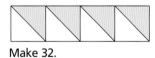

Make 32.

4 Sew a unit from Step 2 to the bottom of each large half-square triangle, with the dark blues touching. Sew a unit from Step 3 to the right side. Make 32 blocks.

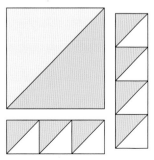

Sew the 3 sections together.

Cheesecloth overlay

1 Prepare Setacolor paint by mixing 4 oz. of paint with 12 oz. of water in a pint jar or other container.

2 Dampen each yard of cheesecloth with water; wring out excess. Scrunch a 1-yard section of cheesecloth on the aluminum tray until it is all on the tray.

3 Use a foam brush to dab paint on the cheesecloth; leave some areas white.

4 Transfer the painted cheesecloth to an outdoor area to dry.
   Tip: If you leave the cheesecloth scrunched while it dries, some of the paint will travel, making darker and lighter areas.

5 Clean tray and repeat with remaining cheesecloth.

6 When all cheesecloth has airdried, put it in a hot dryer with several damp towels to heat-set the paint for 30 minutes.
   Tip: Towels might pick up a small bit of paint; do not use good towels.

QUILT TOP ASSEMBLY

Storm at Sea blocks

1 Sew the blocks into 4 rows of 3 blocks each. Press seams open.

2 Sew the 4 rows together. Press seams open. Your quilt top should measure 36½" x 48½".

Organza clouds

1 Draw cloud shapes on the paper side of fusible web; fuse to the organza. Cut out the cloud shapes.

Tip: Remember that shapes marked on the fusible web backing make mirror images once the organza is cut.

2 Arrange the organza clouds on the quilt top so they soften the cloud areas (purple/lavender shades). Use smaller shapes near the bottom of the sky, larger ones near the top, overlapping the cloud shapes slightly.

3 Fuse the organza clouds to the quilt following the manufacturer's instructions. Be sure to fuse the most underneath layer of clouds first.

4 Use invisible thread in the top of your machine and zigzag-stitch around the edges of the clouds.

Cheesecloth overlay

1 Work outside or in a very well-ventilated area. Use newspaper and masking tape to block off the areas of the quilt top that will not be covered with cheesecloth.

2 Spray the unblocked areas with fabric spray adhesive.

3 Arrange the painted cheesecloth to imitate sea foam. Scrunch to add dimension but allow some quilt top to show through the cheesecloth. Cut as needed.

4 Use invisible thread to zigzag-stitch all outside edges of the cheesecloth.

5 Use a straight machine stitch here and there to hold the cheesecloth "foam" in place.

Tip: Sew slowly so the scrunched cheesecloth does not get hooked over the presser foot.

6 To try the optional bobbin-stitching, change your bobbin case to one that has been filled two-thirds full with iridescent white yarn. Loosen the bobbin case screw slightly until it accommodates the yarn. Attach the darning foot to the machine. Thread the needle with a smooth metallic thread, and use a longer stitch length than usual.

Tip: Adjust or loosen top tension on a practice piece before using on quilt top.

7 Turn the quilt top face down. Stitch large (about 2"–3") circles inside the zigzag stitching which holds the cheesecloth.

8 With a darning or chenille needle, pull the ends of the yarn to the back of the quilt top and tie off; trim.

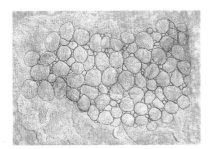

Detail of foam bubble quilting design

9 If necessary, trim the organza and cheesecloth even with the edge of the Storm at Sea blocks.

Lady of the Lake border blocks

1 Sew the 2" x 48½" inner border strips to the sides of the quilt top.

2 Sew 8 border blocks together vertically as shown. Repeat to make 2 side borders.

3 Sew the borders to each side of the quilt. Press seams toward the inner border.

4 Sew 6 border blocks together horizontally. Repeat to make the horizontal top and bottom borders. Add a 2" x 6½" inner border strip to both ends of each. Sew a block to each end of each row as shown.

5 Sew the 2" x 51½" border strips to the top and bottom block borders.

6 Pin the horizontal borders to the top and bottom, matching centers. Sew. Press seams toward the inner border.

FINISHING

See Quilting Basics, page 93, for general quilting and finishing instructions.

1 Layer the quilt top, batting, and backing. Pin-, thread-, or spray-baste.

2 Quilt as desired.

3 Bind.

4 Add a hanging sleeve and label.

Quilt Assembly Diagram

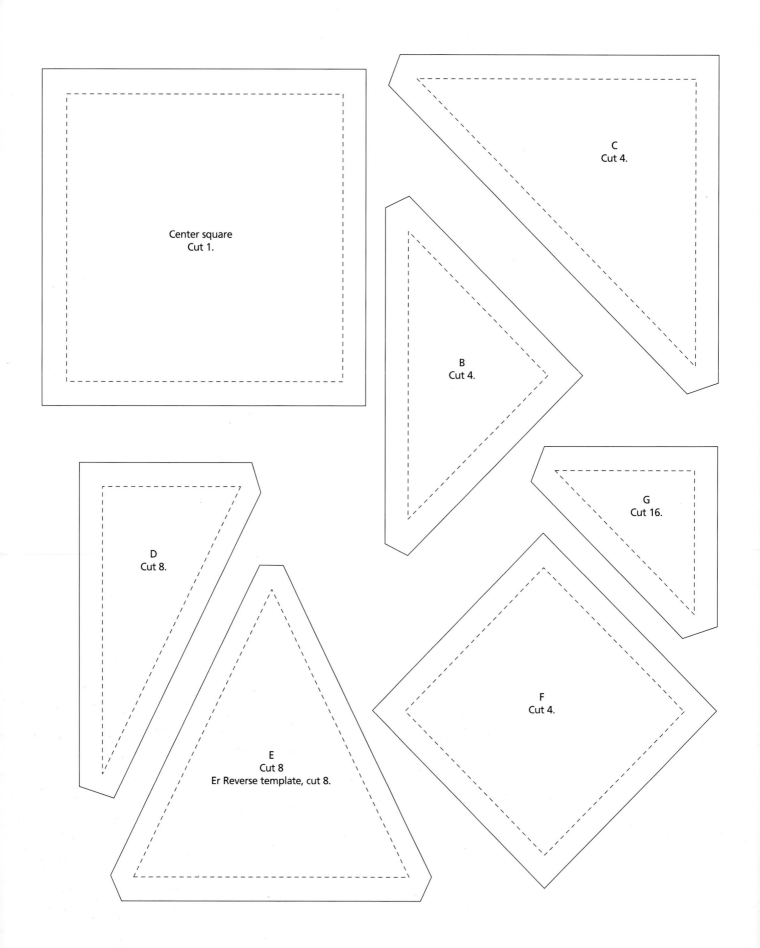

Center square
Cut 1.

C
Cut 4.

B
Cut 4.

G
Cut 16.

D
Cut 8.

E
Cut 8
Er Reverse template, cut 8.

F
Cut 4.

Undersea Reef

55" x 55", Betty Alofs, Lakeside, CA, 2000
Machine pieced, appliquéd, quilted, and embellished.

This quilt was made in a Jan Krentz class and appeared in her book *Lone Stars and Beyond*. I have always loved the ocean, especially the tropical fish, coral, and undersea creatures. After selecting my colors for the star, the quilt grew into a picture of that undersea world. We all gravitate to the sea for its calming influence. Whenever I need to restore my spirits, my quilt takes me there!

pleiades pineapple

Dixie Haywood, Pensacola, FL, and Jane Hall,
Raleigh, NC, 1996. Hand quilted by Sharon
Steele. From the collection of Mary Underhill.
Finished quilt size: 78" x 96"

This stunningly graphic design was created for the raffle quilt for the 1997 International Quilt Festival in Houston, Texas. It pays tribute to the Pleiades, a small cluster of stars in the constellation of Orion. You can create a wallhanging, or a smaller or larger quilt, by varying the number and size of blocks. The pattern is suitable for advanced beginner to intermediate skill levels. It is easiest done by machine on paper or interfacing foundations, but can also be pieced by hand using fabric foundations.

Fabric Requirements

Blue: 21 assorted fat quarters for the pineapple blocks and star block backgrounds

White-on-white: 16 assorted fat quarters for pineapple blocks

Red: 9 assorted fat eighths for star blocks

Red solid: ½ yard for inner border

Navy solid: ½ yard for middle border

Medium blue: 1⅔ yards for outer border

Backing: 6 yards

Batting: 82" x 100"

Binding: ⅝ yard

Other supplies

Tracing paper or lightweight removable interfacing for foundations

Pencil for tracing pattern

Cutting

Pineapple Blocks

For *each* of the 9" x 9" blocks:

Blue: Cut 4 strips 1¼" x 22".

Cut 2 squares 2¾" x 2¾", then cut once diagonally.

Cut one square 2" x 2".

White-on-white: Cut 4 strips 1¼" x 18".

For *each* of the 4½" x 9" half-blocks:

Blue: Cut 2 strips 1¼" x 22".

Cut 1 square 2 ¾" x 2¾", then cut once diagonally.

Cut 1 rectangle 1¼" x 2".

White-on-white: Cut 2 strips 1¼" x 18".

For *each* of the 4½" square quarter-blocks:

Blue: Cut 1¼" square.

Cut 1 strip 1¼" x 22".

Cut 1 square 2¾" x 2¾", then cut once diagonally (you will only need one triangle).

White-on-white: Cut one strip 1¼" x 18".

Stars

Trace the star block patterns on page 34 onto template plastic, adding ¼" seam allowances on all sides. Use the templates to cut the squares, diamonds, and triangles.

For each of the 4⅝" x 4⅝" blocks cut:

Red: 8 diamonds from each of the 9 fat eighths

Blue: 4 squares and 4 triangles each from 9 different blue fat quarters

Borders

Solid red: Cut 8 strips 1" wide for the inner border.

Solid navy: Cut 8 strips 1½" wide for the middle border.

Medium blue: Cut 9 strips 6½" wide for the outer border.

Binding: Cut 9 strips 2" wide by width of fabric.

Block assembly

Pineapple block

Finished size: 9" x 9"

1 Prepare the Pineapple foundations by enlarging the pattern on page 34 to 9½" x 9½". Trace 48 whole blocks onto tracing paper or lightweight interfacing. Trace 28 patterns for the half-blocks and 4 quarter-block patterns. To make patterns for the blocks with star insets, cut strips 10 and 11 from one corner of 12 foundations, and strips 10 and 11 from one corner of 12 foundations, as shown on page 32.

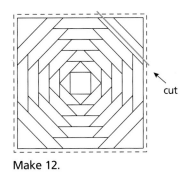

Make 12.

Cut strips 10 and 11 from two opposite corners of 12 foundations as shown.

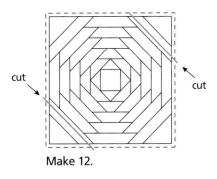

Make 12.

Tip: If you choose a paper foundation, rather than tracing multiple patterns, you can needlepunch the stitching lines by using an unthreaded sewing machine: Use a long stitch length to make perforated stitching lines on up to 10 sheets at a time. (If you feel that you will need the fabric placement lines, use a pencil to draw them in ¼" beyond the stitching line.)

2 Pin or gluestick the center square onto the unmarked side of the foundation, right side up. Raw edges should overlap the stitching lines by ¼".

3 Cut 4 rectangles 2" long from the white strips (the finished size of the center square plus ¼" on each end). Pin the first white piece in place, right side down against the center square, matching the cut edges. Turn the unit over so the paper side is up and the fabric is against the feed dogs, and with a short stitch, sew on the line. Turn the unit over, finger-press the strip open, and pin it in place. Sew the second white strip to the opposite side of the square, pinning it in place on the right side and stitching on the paper side. Follow this procedure to add white strips to the other two sides of the square.

4 The second row of blue strips goes across the diagonal at the corners of the blue center square. Cut 4 rectangles 2" long from the first blue fabric strip. Sew opposite sides in a 1–3, 2–4 sequence.

5 As each row is completed, trim the seam allowances to ¼".

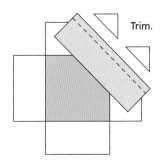

Trim.

Tip: You can pin opposite sides and sew them without removing the foundation from the machine. After the third row of blue strips, it is no longer necessary to piece on opposite sides; you can position, pin, and stitch all four strips in one sewing, hopping from the end of one line to the beginning of the next.

6 Continue to add white strips on the straight rows and blue strips on the diagonal rows.

7 Add the corner pieces as indicated on the foundation.

8 After completing the 48 full blocks, make the 28 half-blocks and the 4 quarter-blocks in the same fashion.

Star block

Finished size: 4⅝" x 4⅝"
Make 9 blocks.

1 Sew red diamonds into pairs.

2 Inset the corner squares.

3 Sew the pairs to one another and inset side triangles.

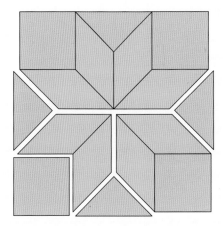

Piecing diagram for stars

QUILT TOP ASSEMBLY

1 Sew the blue-and-white pineapple blocks into rows, using the outside solid line of the foundation as a stitching guide. Set in the Star blocks to the row above, as each row is constructed.

2 Join rows together. Set in the Star blocks to the row below as each row is joined to the one above.

3 With foundations still in place to prevent stretching of the quilt top, add the side inner borders, then the top and bottom borders onto the quilt top.

Star block positioned for setting in.

Quilt Assembly Diagram

4 Add the side middle borders, then the top and bottom middle borders.

5 Add the side outer borders, then the top and bottom outer borders.

6 Carefully remove the foundation material from all the blocks.

FINISHING

See Quilting Basics, page 93, for general quilting and finishing instructions.

1 Layer the quilt top, batting, and backing; baste.

2 In the original quilt, the centers, corners, and inner border were stitched-in-the-ditch. An elongated diamond was quilted in both the blue and the white pineapple designs, and a small four-pointed star was quilted in the large blue corners.

3 Bind.

4 Add a hanging sleeve and label.

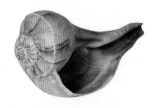

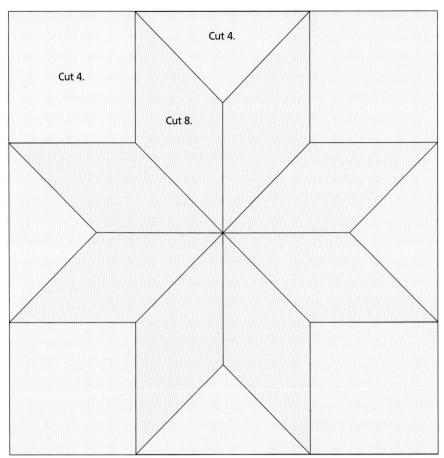

Star block

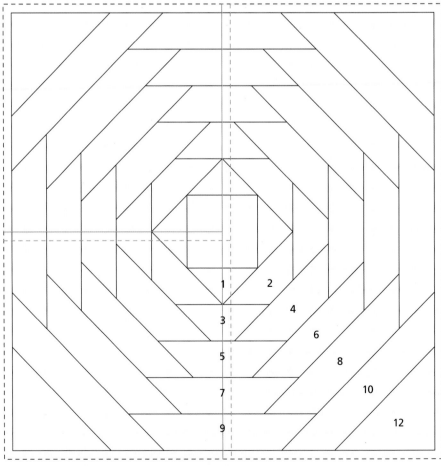

Pineapple foundation pattern. Enlarge 200%. Make 63.

Crooked Tree at Little Boar's Head

42" x 31½", Peg Johnson, Rye, NH, 2002
Collage appliqué.

All I have to do to be inspired to make seascapes is to look out my window! This quilt was inspired while taking photos in September 2000 for a commission quilt. It was such a beautiful day and the sky was gorgeous, so I took several photos. This is the third seascape from those photos and there will be more!

Goin' Fishing

36½" x 33", Linda Papke, Missoula, MT, 2001 Machine appliquéd and quilted.

Otters exude a joy of living, and it seemed natural to make a wallhanging to remind myself to do the same.

Underwater FantaSEA

36" x 28", Lynn L. Gettelfinger,
Rock Hill, SC, 2002
Raw-edge appliqué, free-motion
embroidery, machine quilted.

This quilt is my original design,
inspired by Susan Carlson's book
Free-Style Quilts.

Carpe Diem

79" x 51", Nancy Ota,
San Clemente, CA, 1998
Machine pieced, hand appliquéd,
and machine quilted.

Janet and Russ Landreth commis-
sioned this quilt for their daughter
Noel as a college graduation pres-
ent. Noel is a surfer, lifeguard, and
coach who has traveled extensively
and surfed in many waters. She
sits on the beach contemplating
the vast world before her with her
favorite animals, plants, and the
sea. The quilting depicts the
California State Lifeguard insignia,
and the names of her favorite surfing spots are in the waves. *"Live
while you live and seize the day"*
(Thoreau) is written on the back
of her surfboard and is repeated on
the back of her quilt.

Smooth Sailing

57" x 76", Jackie Robinson, Hesperus, CO, 2001
Machine pieced. Machine quilted by Miklos Champion of Gunter, TX.

I'm a mountain girl and have spent very little time by the ocean, so when this quilt came into "being" it was truly a delight to create. *Pattern available from Animas Quilts, www.animas.com, or P.O. Box 693, Durango, CO 81312.*

Teri Biglands,
Peachtree City, GA, 1996
Finished quilt size:
35" x 52"
Owned by Gail Schrader

The beginnings of Gail's Whale of a Tale lie in a barter I made with my friend Gail's sister: a piece of Gail's stained glass for a quilted wallhanging. The only requirement for the wallhanging was that it should feature Orcas, because Gail is an avid whale watcher. My research led me to the work of Hawaiian artist Christian Riese Lassen. His painting, "Children of the Stars," became my inspiration. I had never designed a quilt before, and because it was a labor of love, it was very difficult for me to let the finished wallhanging go. (However, I knew that it was going to a happy home.) The name for the quilt came about because Gail frequently travels abroad and always returns with fascinating and funny stories to tell. I was thrilled when the quilt was juried into and featured in the 1997 International Quilt Festival in Houston, Texas.

FABRIC REQUIREMENTS

Blues, aquas, and purples: 15 assorted fat quarters for water

Black or navy: ½ yard for foundation

Navy: ½ yard for sky and stars

Black: One yard for whales and sky

Mottled light gray fabric: ¼ yard for whales and stars

Brights: assorted scraps to total ¼ yard for Mariner's Compass

Scrap of mottled dark gray for saddlebags on whales

Backing: 1⅝ yards

Batting: 39" x 56"

Binding: ½ yard

Other supplies

Paper or fabric for foundations

Freezer paper for appliqué

Clear invisible thread

White yarn or cotton thread of similar thickness for embroidery

Silver sequins and clear beads

Size $^{10}/_{13}$ beading needle

Removable fabric marker

CUTTING

Blues, aquas, and purples: Precut the fat quarters into 3"-wide strips; cut 2 strips 4" wide of the lightest values. You will need 147 strips of different lengths; study your enlarged diagram and the quilt photo to make sure you have the correct number of pieces in the required colors and lengths. Paper-pieced shapes should be cut ¾" larger on every side.

All appliqué pieces are cut individually.

Binding: Cut 5 strips 2" wide x width of fabric.

QUILT TOP ASSEMBLY

Background

1 Enlarge the sky and water pattern on page 41. Trace each section onto a separate foundation. Be sure to transfer all registration marks.

2 Cut out the foundations.

3 For foundation-pieced sections, refer to the paper piecing instructions on page 95. Beginning at one end and working your way to the opposite end, sew strips to each of the foundations.

4 After stitching, trim each section to the foundation leaving a ¾" seam allowance. Do not remove the foundations.

5 For sky sections, use each foundation as an individual pattern. On the wrong side of the fabric, draw around the outside edge, transferring all registration marks. Cut out, leaving a ¾" seam allowance.

6 Match registration marks, then stitch all the background sections together.

Tip: Clip the curved seams after sewing. This will help the quilt to lie flat.

7 Remove the paper foundations. Press carefully. At this point you may find it necessary to square your quilt.

Patterns for whales. Enlarge 520%. Cut bodies in black, details in light gray.

Whales

1 Enlarge the patterns above. Trace the outline of each whole whale body, and each white detail, onto the paper side of the freezer paper.

2 Iron the freezer-paper patterns for the whale bodies to the wrong side of the black fabric. Cut out the shapes, adding a ¼" turn-under allowance all around. Repeat with the detail patterns and the mottled gray fabrics, adding a ⅛" seam allowance.

3 Using a dry iron, press the seam allowances to the wrong side of the shape, using the edge of the freezer paper as a pressing guide for a sharp edge. Work on one shape at a time. Clip and notch seam allowances as necessary to allow them to lie flat.

4 Sew the mottled light gray areas to each whale before appliquéing the whale onto the water. Use either the needle-turn hand appliqué method or zigzag stitch by machine.

Tip: You can wrap the seam allowance of the mottled light gray area around the edge of the black whale body and trim away the ⅛" black seam allowance. You will eliminate the bulk of two seam allowances.

5 Refer to the quilt photo for the placement of the whales. Appliqué whales; be sure to insert Whale C under the fin of Whale B before you appliqué the fin.

Mariner's Compass

1 Enlarge the Mariner's Compass pattern on page 42. Trace onto the paper side of freezer paper. Transfer all letters. Cut the freezer-paper templates apart and iron them onto the wrong side of your fabric choices. Cut them out with a ¼" turn-under allowance.

2 Using the freezer paper as a guide, match seams and sew a B patch to each side of each A patch. Press the seams in one direction. Make 16.

3 Sew 2 A/B units to both sides of each C patch. Press seams in one direction. Make 8.

4 Sew 2 A/B/C units to both sides of each D patch. Press seams in one direction. Make 4.

5 Sew each A/B/C/D unit to the left side of each A patch. Press seams in one direction. Make 4.

6 Stitch the quadrants together. Press the seams open.

7 Appliqué the center circle onto the top of the completed compass. Remove the templates.

8 Cut a circle of freezer paper the same size as your finished Mariner's Compass. (Do not include the outer seam allowance.) Iron the freezer paper circle onto the wrong side of the Mariner's Compass. Press the seam allowance to the wrong side, using the edge of the paper as a guide for a sharp edge. Clip as necessary. Baste the turn-under using long stitches.

9 Pin the Mariner's Compass in place onto the quilt top and blindstitch by hand, or use a narrow machine zigzag to stitch in place. Leave 1½" open, and remove the basting stitches and

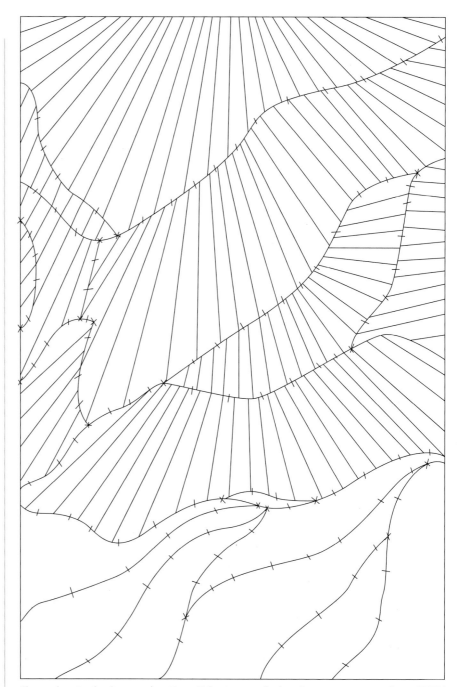

Sky and water background pattern. Take to a professional copy center to enlarge 757%.

freezer paper. Stitch the opening to complete the appliqué.

Stars

1 As in Step 1 of the Mariner's Compass, make freezer-paper patterns for the stars.

2 Cut 24 of C in black, and 24 of B in mottled light gray fabric. Cut 4 of A in blue, using a leftover scrap; repeat 5 times, using a different blue for each set of 4.

3 Sew blue A patches to light gray B patches *along the short*

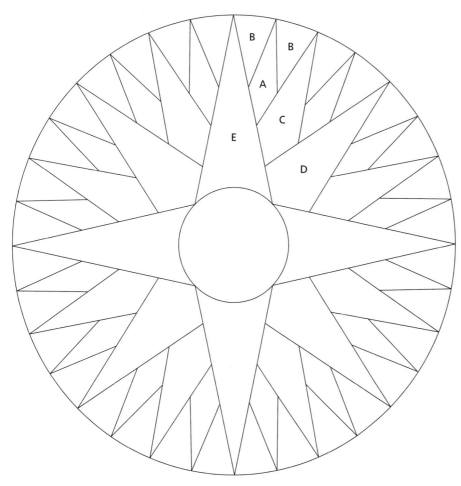

Mariner's Compass pattern. Enlarge 167%.

side, then inset C patches to create 4 quarter-circles. Sew the quarter-circles into pairs. Sew the two pairs together along the center.

4 Clip seam allowances at inside corners and press under. Notch out seam allowances at star points and press flat.

5 Appliqué the six stars in place according to the photo.

FINISHING

See Quilting Basics, page 93, for general quilting and finishing instructions.

1 Layer the quilt top, batting, and backing; baste.

2 For the water portion, stitch-in-the-ditch with invisible thread. Echo-quilt the sky with invisible thread, following the natural curves. The stars and Mariner's Compass are outline-quilted in a metallic silver thread.

3 Bind.

4 Add a hanging sleeve and label.

Embellishments

1 Make French knots above the top whale using the white yarn or thick cotton thread.

2 To attach the sequins, use a size $^{10}/_{13}$ beading needle and a small clear bead to hold them in place. Knot the transparent thread, and pull the knot into the batting to hide it. Thread on a sequin, then a bead, and put the needle back through the center of the sequin. When the first sequin is secure,run the needle through the batting to the next area you would like a sequin and repeat the process. The sequins are sprinkled around the sky in imitation of the constellations.

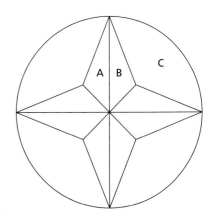

Star pattern. Enlarge 175%.

Balmy Summer Evenings with Possible Fairies

35" x 59", Mary Ellen Parsons, Carmel Valley, CA, 2002. Machine pieced and quilted with hand appliqué.

This wonderful design evolved from my method of working with images and colors in one part of a design and following where the muse leads me. When the lazy, summer evening scene was complete, I felt that it was a little static, that it needed a spark of interest. A whimsical impulse led to the addition of the fairies (five in all—can you find them?), creating an interactive quilt that engages viewers both young and old.

Karen Kent, Marstons Mills, MA, 2000
Finished quilt size: 21" x 21"

This block-of-the-month design represents some of the things I love about summer on Cape Cod. After the last day of school our beach bags are packed and ready to go to the beach whenever the mood strikes.

FABRIC REQUIREMENTS

Blue: ½ yard for background

Woven straw print: 1 fat quarter for beach bag

Hot pink print: ¼ yard (or fat quarter) for flip-flops

Yellow: ⅛ yard for inner border

Purple novelty print: ¼ yard (or fat quarter) for outer border

Scraps: blue-and-red print for flower, green print for leaves, brown or orange print for suntan lotion bottle, white for bottle label, black for bottle cap

Backing: ⅝ yard

Batting: 25" x 25"

Binding: ⅛ yard

Other supplies

Hand appliqué: Freezer paper for tracing patterns

Machine appliqué: ¼ yard fusible web

Permanent marking pens in various colors for drawing suntan lotion label

Ribbon for flip-flops in pale blue or desired color: ½ yard

Small embroidered flower appliqués (pansies are shown) for flip-flops

Large yellow flat button for flower center on bag

Red embroidery floss

Optional: Additional flat buttons for embellishment

CUTTING

Blue background: Cut one 14½" x 14½" square.

Yellow inner border: Cut 2 strips 1" x 14½" for the sides; cut 2 strips 1" x 15½"" for the top and bottom borders.

Purple outer border: Cut 2 strips 3¼" x 15½" for the sides; cut 2 strips 3¼" x 21" for the top and bottom borders.

Woven straw print: Cut a 2½" x 11" strip for the bag handle.

Blue-and-red print for flower: Cut 2 squares 3" x 3".

Green print leaves: Cut 4 rectangles 2" x 4".

Binding: Cut 3 strips 1¼" x fabric width.

QUILT TOP ASSEMBLY

Tip: Before beginning to appliqué, fold the background rectangle in half lengthwise and finger-press; then fold in half crosswise and finger-press. These lightly pressed lines will help you accurately position the appliqué shapes.

1 Before you begin the appliqué, add the side inner border strips, then the top and bottom inner border strips to the background square.

2 Add the side outer border strips, then the top and bottom outer border strips.

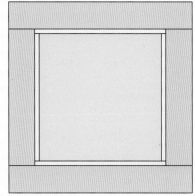

Background with borders added

3 To make the bag handle, fold the woven straw print strip in half lengthwise, right sides together. Stitch ¼" from raw edges down the long side, and turn strip right side out. Press.

4 Prepare for hand or machine appliqué.

Hand appliqué: Enlarge the patterns on page 47. Trace onto the paper side of freezer paper.

Iron the shiny side of the freezer-paper pattern for each shape onto the right side of the fabric. Cut around the patterns, adding a ⅛" turn-under allowance.

Machine appliqué: Enlarge the patterns on page 47. Trace onto the paper side of the fusible web. For a reverse shape (such as the right flip-flop sole or innersole), remember to flip the pattern over. Leave ½" space between shapes. Cut the shapes apart, but do not cut out on the line until after you have fused the web to the fabric. Fuse the web to the wrong side of the fabric following the manufacturer's instructions. Carefully cut each piece on the line.

5 Position the bag handle on the background and pin in place. Fuse or stitch the beach bag in place on the background. Remember to tuck the raw edges of the handle under the top edge of the bag before you fuse or stitch. Tack the handle to the background in several spots.

6 Use a permanent marking pen to draw the design on the suntan lotion label. Do this *before* you attach the label to the bottle (just in case you make a mistake). Copy the photograph (which features an outline of Cape Cod) or make up your own. This is a perfect opportunity to personalize the quilt for its recipient! Next, fuse or stitch the suntan lotion bottle, label, and cap to the quilt top, with the suntan bottle slightly overlapping the bottom corner of the bag.

7 Fuse or stitch the soles of the flip-flops to the quilt top, overlapping the borders and the bag. Pin the innersoles in position on top of the soles.

8 Cut the ribbon into 2 pieces, each 8" long. Fold each in half to form an upside-down "V." Center the point of the folded ribbon on the innersole and tack securely in place. Tuck the ends of the ribbon straps under the innersole before fusing or stitching the innersole in place. Securely stitch the small, embroidered flower appliqués to the "V" of the ribbon straps.

9 To make the three-dimensional flower, fuse the 3" squares, wrong sides together. Trace or pin the flower pattern onto the fused fabric and cut out.

10 Leaves: Follow the steps above to make the two leaves. Arrange the flower and leaves as shown in the photo, then remove the flower so you can tack the upper edges of the leaves to the bag.

11 Use a large yellow button for the flower center. With red embroidery floss, go through the button from the front side, leaving a long thread end. Take a couple of stitches through the button, flower, and quilt top, then cut the thread, leaving another long end. Tie the ends together in a square knot and trim to the desired length.

FINISHING

See Quilting Basics, page 93, for general quilting and finishing instructions.

1 Layer the quilt top, batting, and backing; baste.

2 Stitch-in-the-ditch around all of the shapes, then echo-quilt about ¼"–½" away from the first line of stitching. Quilt the rest of the background as desired: small suns, stipple quilting, or add more lines of echo-quilting.

3 This small wallhanging does not require double-fold binding. Use the 1¼" strips and follow binding instructions on page 94, but do not fold strips in half lengthwise.

4 Add a hanging sleeve and label.

5 If desired, add more buttons in a random design.

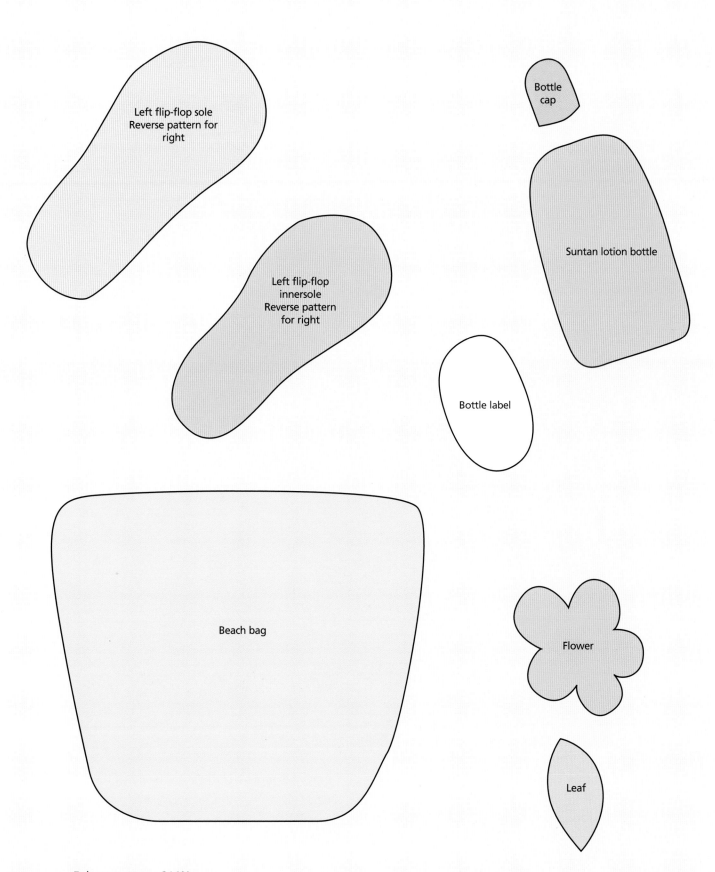

Left flip-flop sole
Reverse pattern for
right

Bottle cap

Suntan lotion bottle

Left flip-flop
innersole
Reverse pattern
for right

Bottle label

Beach bag

Flower

Leaf

Enlarge patterns 214%.

lobster for dinner

Barbara LeBlanc, South Dennis, MA, 2000
Finished quilt size: 20" square

I wanted to make a block for the month of August that represented summertime to me. Boiled lobster dinners are a special favorite of my family. This little quilt represents wonderful food, celebrations with the family, and the good life on vacation at the seashore. So with that thought, Lobster for Dinner was easy to design and fun to make with a seashore print for a border.

FABRIC REQUIREMENTS

Yellow stripe: ½ yard for background

Red check: ½ yard for background

Novelty print: ¼ yard (or fat quarter) for border

White-on-white print: ¼ yard (or fat quarter) for plate and butter dish

Red: ⅛ yard (or fat eighth) for lobster

Scraps of gray print for silverware

Scrap of solid yellow for butter

Backing: ⅝ yard

Batting: 22" square

Binding: ¼ yard

Other supplies

Hand appliqué: Freezer paper

Machine appliqué: ¼ yard fusible web

Permanent marking pen

CUTTING

Yellow stripe: Cut a rectangle 14½" x 5½" for background.

Red check: Cut a rectangle 14½" x 9½" for background.

Novelty print: Cut 2 strips 3¼" x 14½" for the side borders; cut 2 strips 3¼" x 20" for top and bottom borders.

Binding: Cut 3 strips 1¼" x fabric width.

Appliqué shapes are cut individually.

QUILT TOP ASSEMBLY

Tip: Before beginning to appliqué, fold the background square in half lengthwise and finger-press; then fold in half crosswise and finger-press. These lightly pressed lines will help you accurately position the appliqué shapes.

1 With right sides together, sew the yellow stripe and red check background rectangles together to make a 14½" square.

2 Add the side border strips, then the top and bottom border strips.

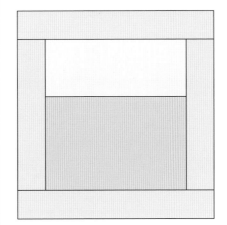

Background with borders.

3 Prepare for hand or machine appliqué.

Hand appliqué: Enlarge the patterns on page 50. Trace onto the paper side of freezer paper. Cut out the freezer paper shapes.

Iron the shiny side of the freezer-paper pattern for each shape onto the right side of the fabric. Cut around the patterns, adding a ⅛" turn-under allowance.

Machine appliqué: Enlarge the patterns on page 50. Trace onto the paper side of the fusible web. Leave ½" space between shapes. Cut the shapes apart but do not cut out on the line until after you have fused the web to the fabric. Fuse the web to the wrong side of the fabric following the manufacturer's instructions. Carefully cut each piece on the line.

4 Center the plate on the red check background fabric and fuse or stitch in place.

5 Use a permanent pen to draw accent lines and numbers on the silverware. On the lobster, draw the eyes, accent lines, and dots.

6 Fuse or stitch the lobster onto the plate. Place the lobster pick and fork to the left of the plate and the knife and spoon to the right and fuse or stitch in place.

7 For the butter dish, fuse or stitch the yellow circle onto the white one; place this above the spoon and fuse or appliqué in place.

FINISHING

See Quilting Basics, page 93, for general quilting and finishing instructions.

1 Layer the quilt top, batting, and backing; baste.

2 Suggestions for quilting include outlining the different shapes and adding steam lines above the lobster and butter. A line of quilting can also be added about ⅝" inside the rim of the plate.

3 This small wallhanging does not require double-fold binding. Use the 1¼" strips and follow binding instructions on page 94, but do not fold strips in half lengthwise.

4 Add a hanging sleeve and label.

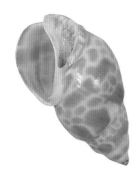

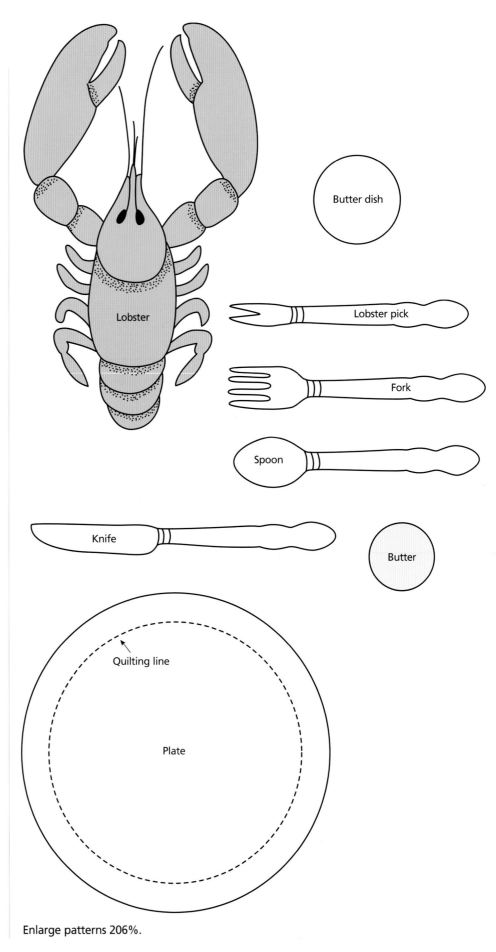

Butter dish

Lobster

Lobster pick

Fork

Spoon

Knife

Butter

Quilting line

Plate

Enlarge patterns 206%.

How I Spent My Summer Vacation

65" x 41", Nancy M. Bales, Skaneateles, NY, 2000
Machine appliqué, free-motion embroidery, machine quilted.

All the senses are alive with the smell and taste of salt water, the scent of wind-worn pines. Hear the splashing and crashing of waves. Feel the warmth of summer!

nantucket
lightship basket

Karen Kent, Marstons Mills, MA, 2000
Finished quilt size: 19" x 20"

Nantucket Lightship baskets feature meticulously hand-carved and inked scrimshaw. The elaborately woven baskets close with ivory fasteners, and are a coveted collector's item. I've always wanted a Lightship basket, and until I can save up for one (they are very expensive), this quilt will have to do.

FABRIC REQUIREMENTS

White or off-white: 1 fat quarter for background

Woven basket or similar novelty print: ¼ yard (or fat quarter) for basket body and lid

Wood print or brown stripe: ¼ yard (or fat quarter) for handle and lid rim

Dark red-brown: ⅛ yard for inner border

Novelty print: ¼ yard (or fat quarter) for outer border

Scraps: dark brown for oval on basket lid and loop closure; muslin for scrimshaw drawing and ivory fastener

Backing: ⅝ yard

Batting: 23" x 24"

Binding: ⅛ yard

Other supplies

Hand appliqué: Freezer paper for tracing patterns

Machine appliqué: ⅓ yard fusible web

Black fine-point permanent marker

Off-white embroidery floss

Two white buttons for basket handle ends

CUTTING

White: Cut a 13½" x 14¾" rectangle for the background.

Dark red-brown: Cut 2 strips 1" x 14¾" for the side inner borders. Cut 2 strips 1" x 14½" for the top and bottom inner borders.

Novelty print: Cut 2 strips 2¾" x 15¾" for side outer borders. Cut 2 strips 2¾" x 19" for top and bottom outer borders.

Binding: Cut 3 strips 1¼" x fabric width.

QUILT TOP ASSEMBLY

Tip: Before beginning to appliqué, fold the background rectangle in half lengthwise and finger-press; then fold in half crosswise and finger-press. These lightly pressed lines will help you accurately position the appliqué shapes.

1 Add the side inner border strips, then the top and bottom inner border strips onto the white rectangle.

2 Add the side outer border strips, then the top and bottom outer border strips.

3 Prepare for hand or machine appliqué.

Hand appliqué: Enlarge the patterns on page 55. Trace onto the paper side of freezer paper. Cut out the freezer-paper shapes.

Iron the shiny side of the freezer-paper pattern for each shape onto the right side of the fabric. Cut around the patterns, adding a ⅛" turn-under allowance.

Machine appliqué: Enlarge the patterns on page 55. Trace onto the paper side of the fusible web. For a reverse shape, remember to flip the pattern over. Leave ½" space between shapes. Cut the shapes apart but do not cut out on the line until after you have fused the web to the fabric. Fuse the web to the wrong side of the fabric following the manufacturer's instructions. Carefully cut each piece on the line.

4 Fuse or stitch the basket pieces in the following order: basket body; lid rim; basket lid (leave 1" open to insert loop closure); handle; oval liner.

5 Draw the scrimshaw design onto the muslin oval with a black fine-point permanent pen, copying the design provided or personalizing the quilt with one of your own. Fuse or stitch in place.

6 To make the loop closure, cut a 1" x 5" bias strip from the brown scrap. Fold the strip right sides together and stitch ¼" from

the cut edges, leaving the ends open. Turn right side out, forming a ¼"-wide tube; trim to 4" long.

7 Make a 2"-long muslin tube in the same way.
The three-dimensional basket closure is made from these two tubes. Stitch the muslin tube in place first, at the center of the upper edge of the basket body; join the ends together to make a circle, then stand the circle up and tack securely in place with tiny stitches.

8 Fold the brown tube into a U-shaped loop; insert the raw ends into the 1" opening that was left when you appliquéd the basket lid in place. Fit the brown loop securely around the standing muslin circle. Stitch securely in place, and close the 1" opening.

9 To finish the fastener, insert the ivory (muslin) stick through the muslin circle, on top of the brown loop, and stitch in place through all layers. This step is best done by hand.

10 Add the "safety" string that attaches the stick to the basket lid by stitching with the off-white embroidery floss.

11 Sew white buttons onto the handle, approximately ½" up from each end.

FINISHING

See Quilting Basics, page 93, for general quilting and finishing instructions.

1 Layer the quilt top, batting, and backing; baste.

2 Stitch-in-the-ditch around all of the shapes, then echo-quilt about ¼"–½" away from the first line of stitching. Quilt the rest of the background as desired: fish, starfish, stipple quilting, or add more lines of echo-quilting.

3 This small wallhanging does not require double-fold binding. Use the 1¼" strips and follow binding instructions on page 94, but do not fold strips in half lengthwise.

4 Add a hanging sleeve and label.

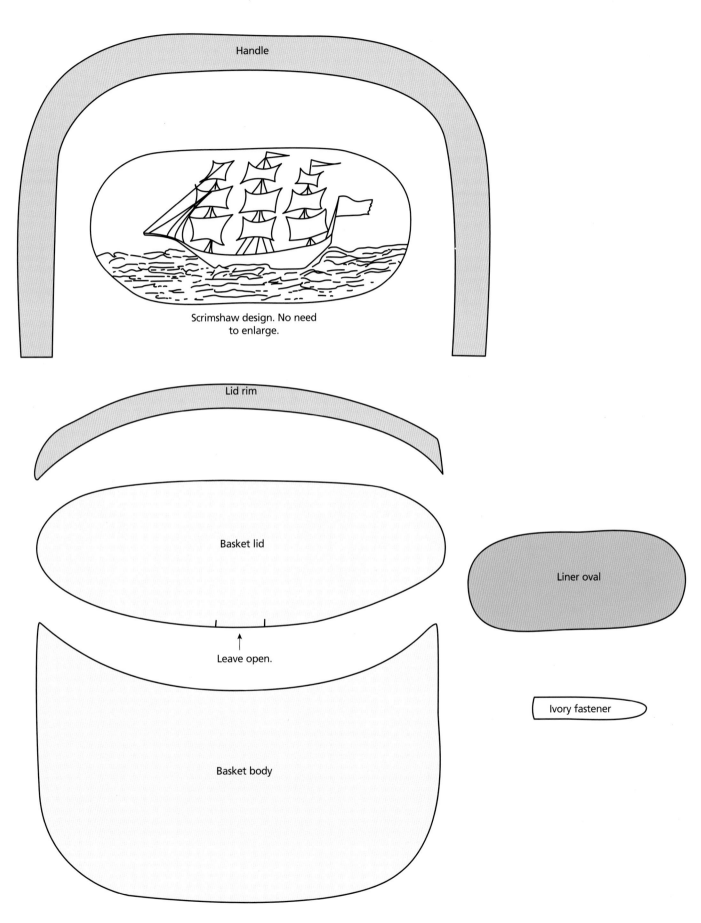

Handle

Scrimshaw design. No need
to enlarge.

Lid rim

Basket lid

Liner oval

Leave open.

Ivory fastener

Basket body

Enlarge patterns 200%.

kissing dolphins

Susan Campbell, Hyannis, MA, 1997
Finished quilt size: 20" x 20"
Options: 44" x 44" wallhanging or 93" x 93" bed quilt

After a trip to Hawaii I was determined to make a Hawaiian-style quilt. I made the quilt for my son Peter, who was in the U.S. Submarine Service, so dolphins were perfect. One very long evening I taped sheets of newsprint together large enough to fit a queen-size bed. I folded the paper into eighths, drew the design, and cut away the background. When I opened the paper I discovered I had reversed the direction of the dolphins. My daughter-in-law, Lisa, quietly commented that she "thought the dolphins were supposed to be kissing." A few hours later the dolphins were kissing, and the quilt had a title. Two years later the 93" x 93" heirloom quilt was finished!

FABRIC REQUIREMENTS

Navy: ¾ yard for top layer

White: ¾ yard for bottom layer

Backing: ¾ yard

Batting: 24" x 24" (thinner is best for smaller quilts, bonded polyester works well on the larger quilts)

Binding: ¼ yard

Options: To make the 44" x 44" wallhanging you will need 1½ yards of each fabric. To make the bed size quilt you would need 8–10 yards of each fabric.

Other supplies

Hand appliqué: Pattern Ease interfacing (or newsprint paper)

Freezer paper

Size 11 straw needles

Machine appliqué: ¾ yard fusible web

Marking pencil or chalk

Paper and embroidery scissors

Thread to match darker fabric

Size 9 quilting needles

Black fine-point permanent pen

PREPARATION FOR REVERSE APPLIQUÉ

Hand appliqué

1 Enlarge the pattern on page 59. Note that the wedge pattern is a one-eighth section of the complete pattern.

2 There are two methods to transfer the design onto the top (darker) layer in preparation for reverse hand appliqué. First, fold the interfacing into eighths as you did in school when making snowflakes: fold in half, then in half again, and then a diagonal fold. Staple the layers together. With permanent pen, copy the design on one wedge. Cut out the design and open the pattern to display the 8 dolphins.

Note: Always cut out the entire pattern before cutting any fabric. Be careful not to cut on the folded edges or your pattern will fall apart!

Fold the navy fabric in half lengthwise, then crosswise, then once more diagonally into a triangular wedge. Lightly finger-press the fold lines so they can be used to position the pattern.

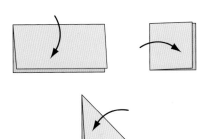

Fold as shown.

Method 1: Lay the pattern on the darker fabric, aligning the fold lines of the pattern with the pressed fold lines on the fabric. Use a chalk marker or silver pencil to trace the pattern directly onto the darker fabric.

Method 2: Trace the master pattern, using permanent pen, onto the dull side of freezer paper. Cut out the freezer-paper pattern.

Iron the shiny side of the freezer-paper pattern onto the right side of the darker fabric. Mark the top with chalk or silver marker and carefully remove the freezer paper. You can also leave the freezer paper on top during the appliqué process; in this case, you do not have to mark the pattern.

3 Fold the light background fabric lengthwise, then crosswise, and once more diagonally into a triangular wedge. Lightly finger-press the fold lines, and then open it on a smooth surface, right side up. Position the navy fabric on top, marked design up, carefully aligning the folds. Following the finger-pressed fold lines, baste horizontally, vertically, and diagonally.

4 Baste around the entire center motif design, ½" outside the marked line or ½" outside the freezer paper pattern.

Tip: In tight areas, one line of basting may be all that is needed.

5 Working in a counter-clockwise direction, and holding your work on the horizontal, start in the center of the motif, cutting away only 3"–4" at a time just ahead of your stitching. Now progress to the

dolphins. Appliqué all 8 tails, then all 8 heads, then all the eyes and flippers. Always use very sharp, pointed scissors. As you cut each shape out, ⅛" to ¼" away from the marked line of the pattern, the white fabric underneath is revealed.

6 Use a ⅛" to ¼" turn-under allowance to stitch the edges of the design in place with small running stitches.

Tip 1: Use a moistened, round wooden toothpick to help turn fabric under; this works better to prevent fraying than needle turning.

Tip 2: Straw needles can be difficult to thread. Wet your thread and the wet the eye of the needle.

Tip 3: To turn under seam allowances in inner V-shaped areas, clip them all the way to the marked line. For outer V-shaped areas, such as points, you need to trim the small triangular flap to reduce the bulk of

the fabric that is turned under. For curved areas, clip to the marked line only on the inner curves; outer curves are smoother without clipping if you maintain a ⅛" turn-under allowance.

7 Continue cutting away and stitching small portions of the design until the entire center motif is revealed.

8 Remove the basting stitches.

9 Now repeat the process with the outer frame blue wave border. Since you cut the center motif out of the fabric, the outer border is in one piece with a big hole in the middle. Gently lay the navy top border on the white background, lining up all the folds and baste. Appliqué, cutting away 3"–4" at a time, leaving ⅛"–¼" seam allowance as you go around the entire perimeter. Remove the basting stitches.

Machine appliqué

1 Enlarge the master pattern. Mark the center lines of the design both horizontally and vertically.

2 Lay the pattern onto the paper side of the fusible web and trace.

3 Following the manufacturer's instructions, fuse the traced design onto the wrong side of the top (darker) fabric.

4 Cut out the entire motif; small scissors help for tight spots. The design will be in two pieces: the first is the 4 pairs of dolphins for the center design, and the second area is the decorative blue border design.

5 Lightly press the center lines lengthwise and crosswise on the white (background) fabric. Spread the background fabric out on a smooth, padded surface suitable for ironing. Working with the outer blue area first, lay it over the background fabric, carefully aligning the outer edges of the two fabrics and matching the center lines horizontally and vertically. Fuse the outer section in place.

6 Carefully place the center motif of the 4 pairs of dolphins in the open white area in the center of the quilt. Fuse in place.

7 Use a narrow zigzag or short straight stitch around all outside edges to secure the top layer and prevent fraying.

FINISHING

See Quilting Basics, page 93, for general quilting and finishing instructions.

1 Layer the quilt top, batting, and backing; baste.

2 Outline stitch-in-the-ditch around the edge of the motif. Then quilt inside the motif, following the outline or making your own design.

3 Next, quilt the background. Echo-quilt from the center, half-way toward the outer wave border. Then echo-quilt from the outer wave border back toward the center, making adjustments to the flow of lines as needed to blend the echo. Echo-quilt about ½" away from the seamline. Add more lines of echo quilting ½" apart. Traditional Hawaiian quilts have quilting lines ½" to ⅝" apart. Trim to finished quilt size.

4 Bind.

5 Add a hanging sleeve and label.

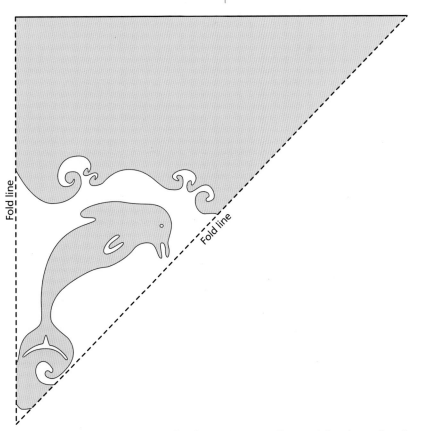

Master pattern. Enlarge 235% for the miniature quilt, 517% for the wall quilt, or 1094% for the bed quilt. The dashed lines are fold lines.

cape cod lobsters

Susan Campbell, Hyannis, MA, 2001
Finished quilt size: 26" x 26"
Options: 44" x 44" wallhanging or 93" x 93" bed quilt

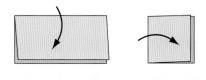

The technique of Hawaiian reverse appliqué, described in detail in Kissing Dolphins, is also used to make Cape Cod Lobsters. It is the second in my series of bed-sized Hawaiian quilts; you can make it in the much smaller, faster-to-finish size. With this quilt I wanted to celebrate my favorite summer meal. Of course, the bright red fabric represents the lobsters after cooking!

As a point of interest, the bodies of the lobsters are quilted to reflect the actual body contours of real lobsters. To have a real, old-fashioned Cape Cod lobster bake we need to add corn-on-the-cob, steamed clams, potatoes, sausage, and seaweed.

FABRIC REQUIREMENTS

Red: ¾ yard for top layer

White: ¾ yard for bottom layer

Backing: ¾ yard

Batting: 30" x 30"

Binding: ¼ yard

Options: To make the 44" x 44" wallhanging you will need 1½ yards of each fabric; to make the bed size quilt you would need 8–10 yards of each fabric.

Other supplies

Hand appliqué: Pattern Ease
   interfacing (or newsprint paper)

Freezer paper

Size 11 straw needles

Machine appliqué: ¾ yard fusible web

Marking pencil or chalk

Paper and embroidery scissors

Thread to match darker fabric

Size 9 quilting needles

Black fine-point permanent pen

PREPARATION FOR REVERSE APPLIQUÉ

Hand appliqué

1 Enlarge the pattern on page 63. Note that the wedge pattern is a one-eighth section of the complete pattern.

2 There are two methods to transfer the design onto the top (darker) layer in preparation for reverse hand appliqué. First, fold the interfacing into eighths as you did in school when making snowflakes: fold in half, then in half again, and then a diagonal fold. Staple the layers together. With permanent pen, copy the design on one wedge. Cut out the design and open the pattern to display the 8 lobsters.

Note: Always cut out the entire pattern before cutting any fabric. Be careful not to cut on the folded edges or your pattern will fall apart!

Fold the red fabric in half lengthwise, then crosswise, then once more diagonally into a triangular wedge. Lightly finger-press the fold lines so they can be used to position the pattern.

Fold as shown.

Method 1: Lay the pattern on the darker fabric, aligning the fold lines of the pattern with the pressed fold lines on the fabric. Use a chalk marker or silver pencil to trace the pattern directly onto the darker fabric.

Method 2: Trace the master pattern, using permanent pen, onto the dull side of freezer paper. Cut out the freezer-paper pattern.

Iron the shiny side of the freezer-paper pattern onto the right side of the darker fabric. Mark the top with chalk or silver marker and carefully remove the freezer paper. You can also leave the freezer paper on top during the appliqué process; in this case, you do not have to mark the pattern.

3 Fold the light background fabric lengthwise, then crosswise, and once more diagonally into a triangular wedge. Lightly finger-press the fold lines, and then open it on a smooth surface, right side up. Position the red fabric on top, marked design up, carefully aligning the folds. Following the finger-pressed fold lines, baste horizontally, vertically, and diagonally.

4 Baste around the entire center motif design, ½" outside the marked line or ½" outside the freezer paper pattern.

Tip: In tight areas, one line of basting may be all that is needed.

5 Working in a counter-clockwise direction, and holding your work on the horizontal, start in the center of the motif, cutting away only 3"– 4" at a time just ahead of your stitching. Now progress to the dolphins. Appliqué all 8 tails, then all 16 claws and 8 heads. Always use very sharp, pointed scissors. As you cut each shape out, ⅛"–¼" away from the marked line of the pattern, the white fabric underneath is revealed.

6 Use a ⅛" to ¼" turn-under allowance to stitch the edges of the design in place with small running stitches.

Tip 1: Use a moistened, round wooden toothpick to help turn fabric under; this works better to prevent fraying than needle turning.

Tip 2: Straw needles can be difficult to thread. Wet your thread and the eye of the needle.

Tip 3: To turn under seam allowances in inner V-shaped areas, clip them all the way to the marked line. For outer V-shaped areas, such as points, you need to trim the small triangular flap to reduce the bulk of the fabric that is turned under. For curved areas, clip to the marked line only on the inner curves; outer curves are smoother without clipping if you maintain a ⅛" turn-under allowance.

7 Continue cutting away and stitching small portions of the design until the entire center motif is revealed.

8 Remove the basting stitches.

9 Now repeat the process with the outer frame blue wave border. Since you cut the center motif out of the fabric, the outer border is in one piece with a big hole in the middle. Gently lay the red top border on the white background, lining up all the folds, and baste. Appliqué, cutting away 3"–4" at a time, leaving ⅛"–¼" seam allowance as you go around the entire perimeter. Remove the basting stitches.

Machine appliqué

1 Enlarge the master pattern on page 63. Mark the center lines of the design both horizontally and vertically.

2 Lay the pattern onto the paper side of the fusible web and trace.

3 Following the manufacturer's instructions, fuse the traced design onto the wrong side of the top (darker) fabric.

4 Cut out the entire motif; small scissors help for tight spots. The design will be in two pieces: one will consist of the 4 large and 4 smaller lobsters that make the center design, and the second area is the decorative red border design.

5 Lightly press the center lines lengthwise and crosswise on the white (background) fabric. Spread the background fabric out on a smooth, padded surface suitable for ironing. Working with the outer red area first, lay it over the background fabric, carefully aligning the outer edges of the two fabrics and matching the center lines horizontally and vertically. Fuse the outer section in place.

6 Carefully place the center motif of the 8 pairs of smaller and larger lobsters in the open white area in the center of the quilt. Fuse in place.

7 Use a narrow zigzag or short straight stitch around all outside edges to secure the top layer and prevent fraying.

FINISHING

See Quilting Basics, page 93, for general quilting and finishing instructions.

1 Layer the quilt top, batting, and backing; baste.

2 Outline stitch-in-the-ditch around the edge of the motif. Then quilt inside the motif, following the outline or making your own design.

3 Next, quilt the background. Echo-quilt from the center, halfway toward the outer wave border. Then echo-quilt from the outer wave border back toward the center, making adjustments to the flow of lines as needed to blend the echo. Echo-quilt about ½" away from the seamline. Add more lines of echo quilting ½" apart. Traditional Hawaiian quilts have quilting lines ½" to ⅝" apart. Trim to finished quilt size.

4 Bind.

5 Add a hanging sleeve and label.

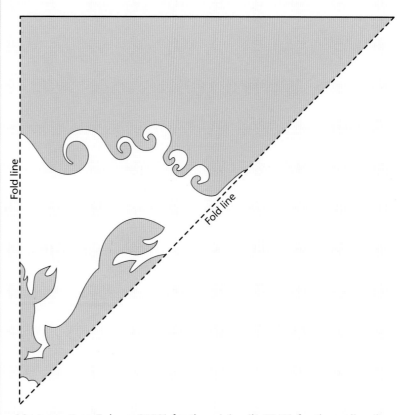

Master pattern Enlarge 315% for the mini quilt, 534% for the wall quilt, or 1027% for the bed quilt. The dashed lines are fold lines.

Mickey Depre, Oak Lawn, IL, 2000
Finished quilt size: 67½" x 87½"

This quilt celebrates my son's love of the ocean and all things in it. The traditionally pieced Lost Ships blocks provide a backdrop for Pauli's Ocean View. Be sure to "pop" the cork on the bottle and leave a message!

FABRIC REQUIREMENTS

Cream print: one yard for blocks and sand

Bright scraps: 24 pieces at least 6" x 6" for blocks

Fish: 1⅝ yards

Sky blue: 1 yard

Light, medium, and dark blue to green: fat quarters and scraps to equal 3¼ yards for blocks

Tans, beiges, and browns: fat quarters and scraps to total 1½ yards for sand and island

Yellows and oranges: fat quarters and scraps to total ½ yard for sun and appliqué

Backing: 5 yards

Batting: 72" x 92"

Binding: ½ yard

Other supplies

Decorative threads

Fusible web

Fusible fabric interfacing

Black fine-point permanent marker

5" piece of string, twine, or embroidery floss

Freezer paper (optional)

CUTTING

Cream print: Cut 9 strips 2⅞", then crosscut 120 squares 2⅞" x 2⅞". Cut 24 squares diagonally once for blocks.

Bright scraps: Cut 4 squares 2⅞" x 2⅞" from each color, then cut diagonally once for blocks.

Fish fabric: Cut 3 strips 6⅞", then crosscut 12 squares 6⅞" x 6⅞". Cut the squares diagonally once for blocks.

Light, medium, and dark blue to green: Cut 12 squares 10⅞" x 10⅞", then cut diagonally once for blocks.

Cut 38 strips 1½" x 10½" for sashing.

Cut 15 squares 1½" x 1½" for cornerstones.

Cut 170 rectangles 4½" x 2½" for borders.

Tans, beiges, and browns: Cut 135–140 rectangles 4½" x 2½" for borders.

Binding: Cut 8 strips 2" x width of fabric.

All appliqué pieces are cut individually.

BLOCK ASSEMBLY

Lost Ships block

Finished size: 10" x 10"

1   For each block, layer 4 bright scrap 2⅞" squares with 4 cream print 2⅞" squares. Draw a diagonal line from corner to corner. Sew ¼" away from the line on both sides.

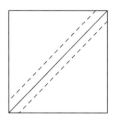

Sew on both sides of the line.

2   Cut on the line to create 8 half-square triangle units. (You will only need 7.)
Repeat with all 24 bright scraps.

Cut on the line.

3   Sew 3 half-square triangle units and one cream print triangle together.

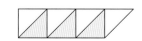

Sew half-square triangles together.

4 Sew 4 half-square triangle units and one cream print triangle together.

5 Sew the 3-unit row to the top and the 4-unit row to the left side of a fish triangle as shown.

6 Sew to a large blue triangle as shown. Make 24.

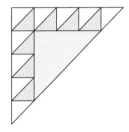

7 Place the completed blocks, sashing, and cornerstones on the design wall. Rearrange them until you are happy with your design.

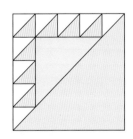

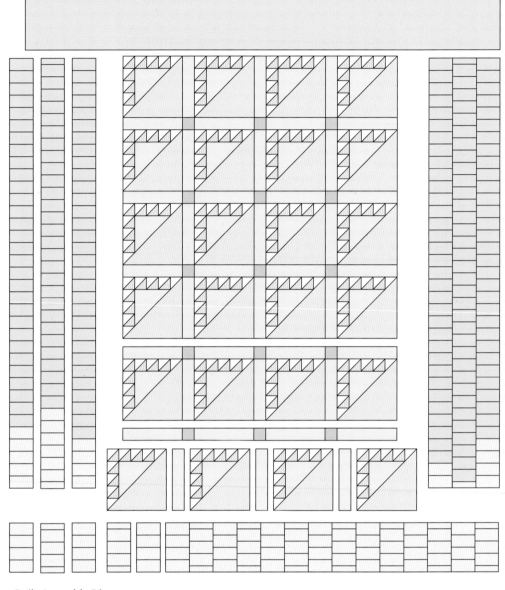

Quilt Assembly Diagram

QUILT TOP ASSEMBLY

1 Sew completed blocks into 6 rows of 4 blocks each, separated by blue sashing strips.

2 Beginning with a sashing strip and alternating with the sashing cornerstones, sew five sashing strips together.

3 Sew the rows of blocks together with the sashing/cornerstone strips as shown in the Quilt Assembly Diagram. Return to the design wall.

4 Referring to the quilt photo, place the 4½" x 2½" blue and green rectangles on the design wall in 3 vertical rows on each side of the quilt center. Offset every other row. Add brown 4½" x 2½" rectangles to the bottom for about 10". Rearrange them until you like your design.

5 Sew the rectangles into vertical rows. Sew the three rows on either side of the quilt top center together. Sew the bottom strips into a rectangle. Sew the side sections to the quilt. Sew the bottom section to the quilt.

6 Measure the width of the quilt top (approximately 67"). Cut or piece the sky fabric to the 12" x width required. Sew the sky to the top of your quilt.

7 If necessary, trim and square the quilt. Return to the design wall.

Appliqué

Free-hand cut large shapes such as the island and water. Free-hand cut or enlarge detail patterns at right. Use your preferred appliqué method to attach the shapes.

1 Refer to the quilt photo on page 64 and arrange random water shapes. Add the island and tree. Appliqué all shapes in place.

Enlarge 950% or as desired.

2 As with the water shapes, position the sand shapes. Add the coral, kelp, fish, and bottles. Appliqué the shapes in place.

3 To create the message in a bottle, write your secret message with the permanent pen onto a piece of fusible fabric interfacing. Cut the message to a square or rectangle. Cut a second piece of fusible fabric interfacing to the same dimensions.

4 Iron fusible web to the wrong side of a scrap of brown or tan "cork" fabric. Fold in half with wrong sides together and cut out a cork shape.

5 Place one end of the string or embroidery floss between the

Add your own message in a bottle.

two cork shapes and the other end between the two message pieces and iron both to fuse the string inside.

Appliqué a small scrap of bottle fabric behind the bottle neck and opening. Appliqué the bottle on top, leaving the lip of the bottle open. Gently fold the lip of the bottle under and slip stitch, without catching the fabric behind. Roll the message into a small tube, and insert into the bottle, leaving the cork and most of the string out.

FINISHING

See Quilting Basics, page 93, for general quilting and finishing instructions.

1 Layer the quilt top, batting, and backing; baste.

2 Quilt as desired.

3 Bind.

4 Add a hanging sleeve and label.

St. Michael's Lighthouse

46¼" x 29¼", Susa C. Kessler,
Baltimore, MD, 2002
Machine pieced and appliquéd.

Many years ago, my son Jack took
a photo of the lighthouse near
St. Michael's in the Chesapeake Bay
on a stormy day while we were sailing.
I have always liked that photo and
have wanted to make a quilt of this
scene for years. However, the techniques I had learned simply didn't
work for this quilt. In a workshop
with Ruth McDowell I learned the
piecing technique I used for this
quilt, and I am happy with the result.

Pier Fun

42" x 24", Nancy Ota, San Clemente, CA, 1995
Machine pieced, hand appliquéd and quilted.

This quilt was inspired by a greeting card design by Woodleigh Hubbard, who drew
carefree, whimsical cats playing and fishing on a pier. This wallhanging is my effort
to capture that spirit of play, and meet the Beach Cities Quilters Guild challenge; it
was my first attempt with the bargello technique.

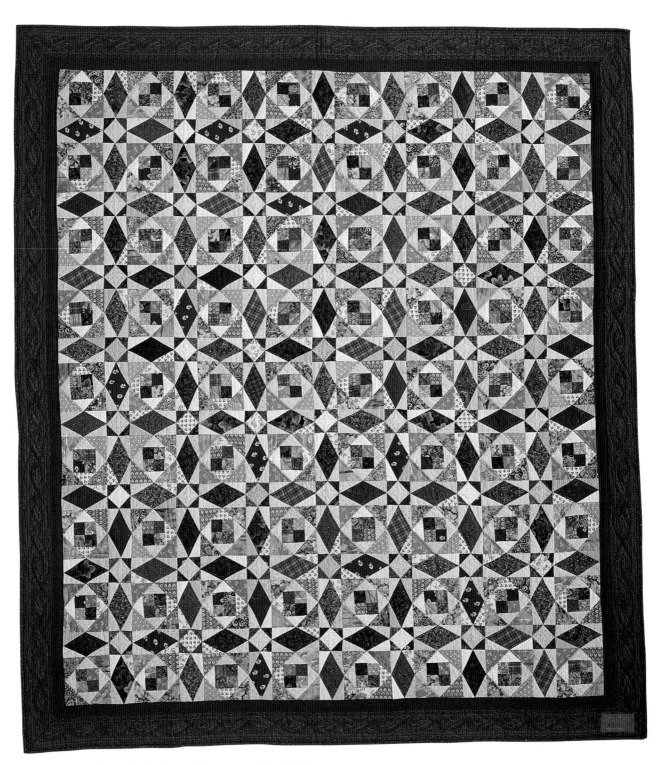

Rosemary Gabriel Wickham, Norcross, GA, 1991
Finished quilt size: 80½" x 89½"

I made Stars at Sea *during my junior year of college; completed in 1991, it was my second quilt. I combed through a number of books and magazines to find examples of the traditional Storm at Sea pattern, and finally selected this one because I liked the little four-patch block in the center of each square. I was delighted when it was given a Viewers' Choice award at a quilt show sponsored by the Mountain Laurel Quilt Guild at my alma mater, Appalachian State University. Subsequently, also at Appalachian State,* Stars at Sea *took first place in an art contest for the Alpha Chi honorary society.*

FABRIC REQUIREMENTS

Light blue, green, and purple prints: assorted scraps, fat quarters, or fat eighths to total 4¼ yards for piecing blocks

Dark blue, green, and purple prints: assorted scraps, fat quarters or fat eighths to total 5 yards for piecing blocks and sashing

Navy: ½ yard for inner border

Green print: 1¼ yards for outer border and binding

Backing: 5¼ yards

Batting: 84" x 93"

Binding: ⅝ yard

CUTTING

Cut all pieces for paper-piecing ½"–¾" larger on all sides than the actual shape. Pieces do not have to be precut; you can cut as you sew each block together.

Light blue, green, and purple prints:

Center four-patch units: For a totally scrappy look (as shown here), cut 144 light print squares 2" x 2".

Quicker option for making four-patches: This will result in a slightly less scrappy look, but makes construction of the four-patches much faster.

Cut 2" strips from 13 light prints and 13 dark prints. Pair each light strip with a dark strip, right sides together. Stitch each pair along one long side, press the seam allowances to the dark fabric, then cut each sewn pair into 3½" units. Randomly pair the 3½" units, then sew four-patch units together, matching light squares to dark squares.

Cut 288 small triangles for the Double Square-within-a-Square blocks.

Cut 508 triangles for the Diamond-within-a-Rectangle blocks.

Cut 56 squares for the Square-within-a-Square blocks.

Dark blue, green, and purple prints:

Center four-patch units: For a totally scrappy look (as shown here), cut 144 dark print 2" x 2" squares.

Cut 127 diamonds for the Diamond-within-a-Rectangle blocks.

Cut 224 triangles for the Square-within-a-Square blocks.

Cut 228 triangles for the Double Square-within-a-Square blocks.

Navy inner border: Cut 8 strips 2" x width of fabric and seam together end-to-end to obtain a length of approximately 302". Cut two 78½" strips for side inner borders. Cut 2 strips 72½" long for top and bottom inner borders.

Green print outer border: Cut 8 strips 4½" x width of fabric and seam together end-to-end. Cut two strips 81½" long for side outer borders. Cut two strips 80½" long for the top and bottom outside borders.

Binding: Cut 9 strips 2" x width of fabric.

BLOCK ASSEMBLY

See General Instructions, page 95, for paper-piecing guidelines.

1 Trace or photocopy the foundation piecing patterns in the following quantities from the patterns on page 73.
72 Double Square-within-a Square blocks
127 Diamond-within-a-Rectangle blocks
56 Square-within-a Square

2 Make 72 small four-patch units for the center of the Double Square-within-a-Square blocks by following the quick-piecing option on page 71, or by sewing a light square to a dark square, then two pairs of light/dark squares together.

3 On the unprinted side of the paper-piecing pattern, align the center of the pieced four-patch unit with the center of the paper pattern. Pin in place. Paper-piece the remaining pieces in numerical order. Make 72 of the Double Square-within-a-Square blocks with the four-patch centers.

4 Paper-piece 127 Diamond-within-a-Rectangle blocks in numerical order.

5 Paper-piece 56 smaller Square-within-a-Square blocks in numerical order.

6 Remove the paper from all of the blocks.

QUILT TOP ASSEMBLY

1 Alternate 8 of the larger Double Square-within-a-Square with 7 of the Diamond-within-a-Rectangle blocks set vertically. Refer to the quilt photo for block placement. Make 9 rows.

2 Alternate 8 of the Diamond-within-a-Rectangle blocks set horizontally with 7 of the smaller Square-within-a-Square blocks. Refer to the quilt photo for block placement. Make 8 rows.

3 Alternate the rows and join together.

4 Add the side inner borders, then the top and bottom inner borders. Press the seam allowances toward the borders.

5 Add the side outer borders, then the top and bottom outer borders. Press the seam allowances toward the borders.

FINISHING

See Quilting Basics, page 93, for general quilting and finishing instructions.

1 Layer the quilt top, batting, and backing; baste.

2 Quilt as desired.

3 Bind.

4 Add a hanging sleeve and label.

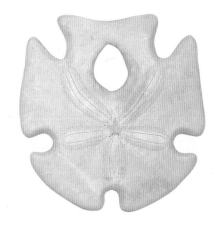

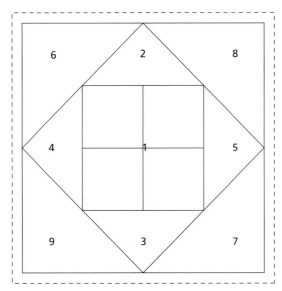

Double Square-within-a-Square block.
Enlarge 231%.

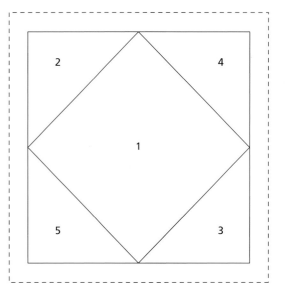

Square-within-a-square block. Enlarge 124%.

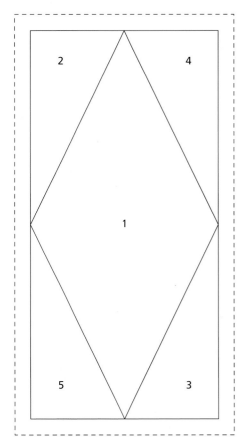

Diamond-within-a-Rectangle block.
Enlarge148%.

Quilt Assembly Diagram

Shore Leave in San Diego

72" x 99", Canyon Quilters of San Diego, CA 2002
Machine pieced background, hand appliqué, machine quilted by Kathy Sandbach.

This stunning quilt, which also features Storm at Sea blocks, was designed and made by the members of Canyon Quilters of San Diego. It depicts the beautiful coastline of San Diego, and features a variety of birds that can be seen in the area.

The Bikini Quilt: Boobs and Bellybuttons

48" x 68", Ami Simms ©1993, pieced and appliquéd, machine quilted.

The Bikini Quilt was originally made as an illustration of triangular patchwork for an article in *Threads Magazine* (August/Sept. 1993). When I suggested it, the editors were less than enthusiastic. Their skepticism, however, just motivated me all the more to make the quilt. The block is called "Hourglass" and was first published in *Classic Quilts: Patchwork Designs from Ancient Rome*, although the quilt in the book bears little resemblance to "Bikini" because the original block is flipped 90°. Every time I looked at the original Roman design I wanted to turn it sideways because it looked just like a bunch of bikini tops. My mother nicknamed this quilt *Boobs and Bellybuttons*; just imagine, the only time in my life I get to have cleavage is when I quilt it! *Contact Ami at www.AmiSimms.com. for the pattern.*

a day at the beach

Flavin Glover, Auburn, AL, 1998
Finished quilt size: 91" x 70½"

*For more pictorial Log Cabin quilt projects,
look for Flavin Glover's C&T book, tentatively titled
Pictorial Log Cabins, in Fall 2003.*

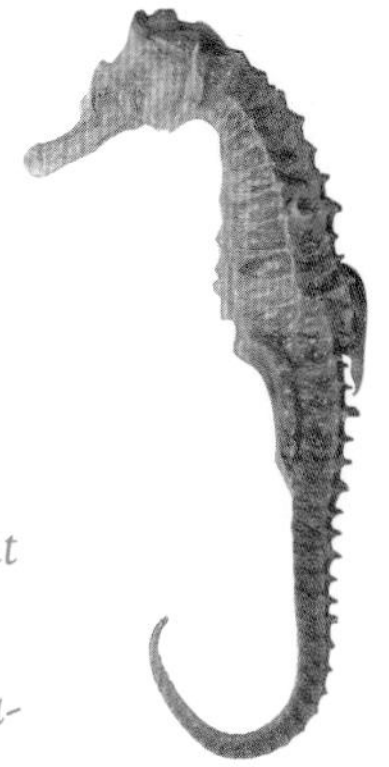

As I flipped through a catalog one day, a beach umbrella lying open on a sandy beach caught my eye. Being a quilter, the umbrella looked like a patchwork Kaleidoscope block to me.
Before I lost the vision, I quickly found my art supplies and colored a line of umbrellas lying on a beach against a background of blue sky. I initially thought of them as a potential border for a sailboat quilt. However, in the next Sunday paper's coupon section, a colorful yogurt ad inspired a complete design. It showed a stylized scene of sea, sailboats, and sky, with colorful yogurt cartons sitting on the beach. I thought "Why not replace the yogurt cartons with beach umbrellas?"
The umbrellas and sun are made from Kaleidoscope blocks. The rest of the design is composed of a combination of rectangular and square Courthouse Steps Log Cabin blocks.

Fabric Requirements

Striped and checked fabrics work well for the umbrellas; bright solids work as well.

Stripes, checks, or solids: assorted fat quarters or fat eighths to total 1¾ yards for umbrellas

Sandy tans and beiges: assorted lights, mediums, and darks to total 2¼ yards for beach

Navy, blues, and blue-grays: assorted lights, mediums, and darks to total 3½ yards for sea and sky

Bright yellow: fat eighths or scraps for sun

Dark red: fat eighths or scraps for sailboat hull

Solid white: assorted tone-on-tones to total ¼ yard for sails (try using cotton brocades for varied texture)

Border: ⅞ yard of gray solid

Batting: 74" x 94"

Backing: 6 yards

Binding: ⅝ yard of black-and-white striped fabric

Cutting

Kaleidoscope blocks

Using pattern A and B on page 81, cut stripes, checks, or solids for each umbrella and the sun block.

Cut 8 A's for each block.

Cut 4 B's for each block.

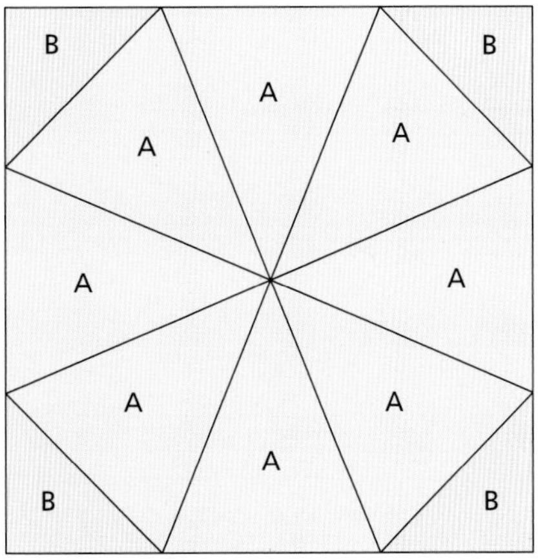

Kaleidoscope block

Note: The cutting instructions that follow for all of the Log Cabin blocks are for traditional piecing. The strip lengths do not have to be precut.

Rectangular Courthouse Steps Log Cabin blocks

Blocks needed: 44 beach, 22 sea, and 58 sky

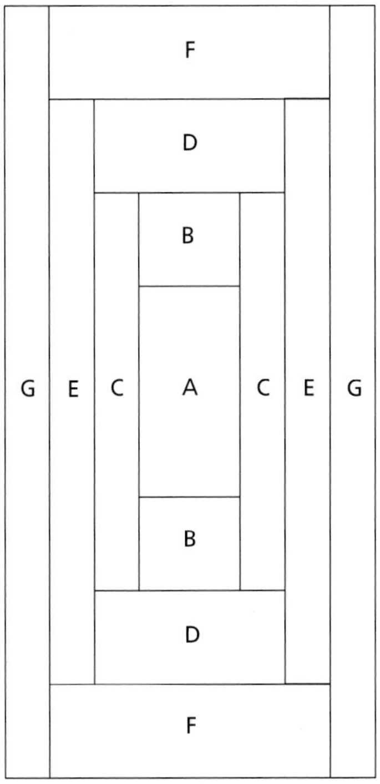

Rectangular Courthouse Steps Log Cabin block for Background Blocks

Background Blocks

Number to Cut	*Log*	*Width*	*Length*
1	A	1⅝"	2¾"
2	B	1⅝"	1½"
2	C	1"	4¾"
2	D	1½"	2⅝"
2	E	1"	6¾"
2	F	1½"	3⅝"
2	G	1"	8¾"

Square Courthouse Steps Block

Blocks needed: 2 sea, 11 sky

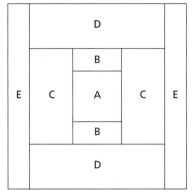

Square Log Cabin block for background blocks

Square Blocks

Number to Cut	Log	Width	Length
1	A	1⅝"	1⅝"
2	B	1"	1⅝"
2	C	1½"	2⅝"
2	D	1½"	3⅝"
2	E	1"	4⅝"

Sailboat Blocks

Each sailboat is individually constructed. Block diagrams follow to clarify variations in piecing order. These also illustrate how to vary log arrangements to achieve the necessary shapes, yet maintain consistent block size.

Left Large Sailboat Block

	Number to cut	Log	Width	Length
Sky Fabric	1	A	1¾"	1¾"
	1	D	1"	2¾"
	1	E	1"	3¼"
	1	H	1"	4¼"
	1	I	1"	4¾"
	1	L	1"	5¾"
	1	M	1"	6¼"
	1	P	1"	7¼"
	1	Q	1"	7¾"
	1	T	1½"	8¾"
Sail Fabric	1	B	1¾"	1½"
	1	C	1½"	2¾"
	1	F	1½"	3¼"
	1	G	1½"	4¼"
	1	J	1½"	4¾"
	1	K	1½"	5¾"
	1	N	1½"	6¼"
	1	O	1½"	7¼"
	1	R	1½"	7¾"
	1	S	1½"	8¾"

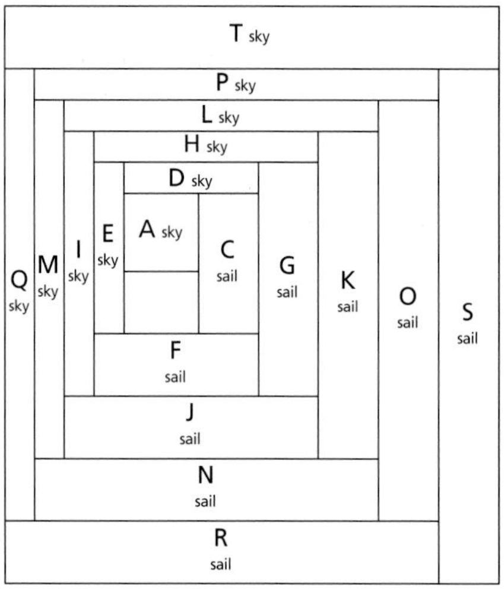

Large Sailboat Left Block

Right Large Sailboat Block

	Number to cut	Log	Width	Length
Sky Fabric	1	A	1⅝"	2¾"
	1	B	1⅝"	1½"
	1	C	1"	4¾"
	1	D	1½"	2⅝"
	1	E	1"	6¾"
	1	F	1½"	3⅝"
	1	G	1"	7¾"
	1	Gc	1"	1½"
	1	H	1½"	4⅝"
Sail Fabric	1	B	1⅝"	1½"
	1	C	1"	4¾"
	1	D	1½"	2⅝"
	1	E	1"	6¾"
	1	F	1½"	3⅝"
	1	G	1"	8¾"

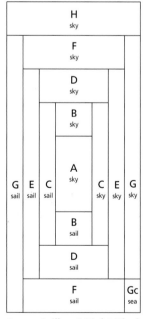

Large Sailboat Right Block

Large Sailboat Bottom (Boat) Block

	Number to Cut	Log	Width	Length
Boat Fabric	1	A	1"	9⅞"
	1	C	1"	10⅞"
	1	E	1"	11⅞"
	1	G	1"	12⅞"
Sea Fabric	2	B	1"	1"
	2	D	1"	1½"
	2	F	1"	2"
	1	G	1"	12⅞"
Sail Fabric	1	H	1⅛"	12⅞"

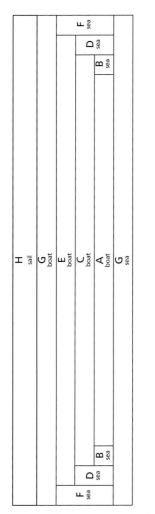

Large Sailboat Bottom Block

Horizon Sailboat 1, Left Block

Note: The left and right block log lengths are the same, but the right block is a mirror image of the left block so the E and G sail logs meet in the middle.

	Number to cut	Log	Width	Length
Sail Fabric	1	A	1"	1¾"
	1	B	1"	1½"
	1	C	1"	3¼"
	1	D	1½"	2½"
	1	E	1"	5¼"
	1	F	1½"	3½"
Sky Fabric	1	A	1"	1¾"
	1	B	1¼"	1½"
	1	C	1"	3¼"
	1	D	1½"	2½"
	1	E	1"	5¼"
	1	F	1½"	3½"
	1	G	1¼"	7¼"
	1	H	1½"	4¾"
	1	I	1"	4¾"
	1	J	1"	8¾"

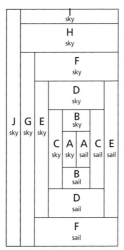

Horizon Sailboat 1, Left Block

Horizon Sailboat 1, Right Block

	Number to cut	Log	Width	Length
Sail Fabric	1	A	1"	1¾"
	1	B	1"	1½"
	1	C	1"	3¼"
	1	D	1½"	2¼"
	1	E	1"	5¼"
	1	F	1½"	3½"
	1	G	1¼"	7¼"
Sky Fabric	1	A	1"	1¾"
	1	B	1¼"	1½"
	1	C	1"	3¼"
	1	D	1½"	2½"
	1	E	1"	5¼"
	1	F	1½"	3½"
	1	G	1¼"	7¼"
	1	H	1½"	4¾"
	1	I	1"	4¾"

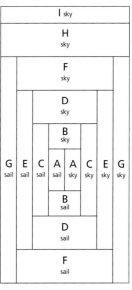

Horizon Sailboat 1, Right Block

Horizon Sailboat 2, Left and Right Blocks

Note: The left and right block log lengths are the same, but the right block is a mirror image of the left block so the G sail logs meet in the middle.

	Number to cut	*Log*	*Width*	*Length*
Sail Fabric	1	A	1"	1¼"
	1	B	1¼"	1⅝"
	1	C	1"	2¾"
	1	D	1½"	2⅝"
	1	E	1"	5¾"
	1	F	1½"	3⅝"
	1	G	1¼"	7¾"
Sky Fabric	1	A	1⅛"	1¼"
	1	B	1¼"	1⅝"
	1	C	1"	2¾"
	1	D	1½"	2⅝"
	1	E	1"	5¾"
	1	F	1½"	3⅝"
	1	G	1"	7¾"
	1	H	1½"	4⅝

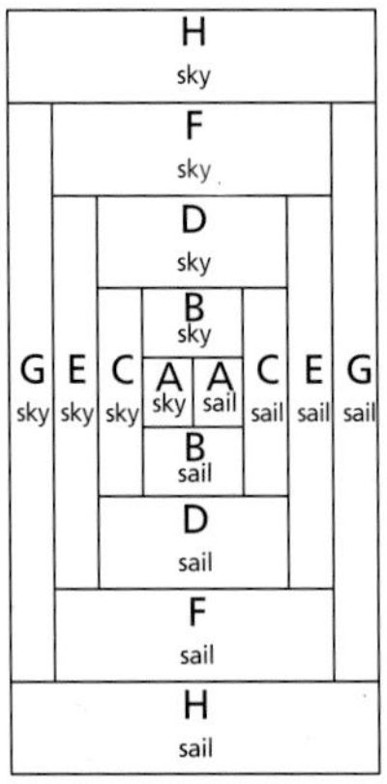

Horizon Sailboat 2, Left Block

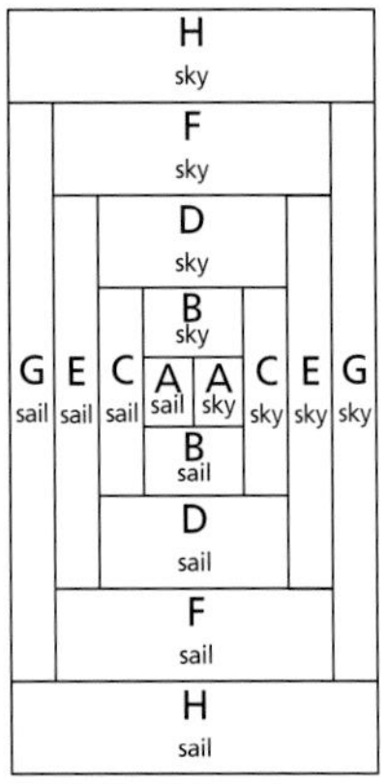

Horizon Sailboat 2, Right Block

Borders: Cut 9 strips 2 1/2"

Binding: Cut 9 strips 1 1/2".

Block Assembly

Kaleidoscope Blocks (8¾" square unfinished)

Blocks needed: 7 umbrellas with
2 tan B's and 2 sea B's
6 umbrellas with tan B's

1 Using the piecing diagram as a guide, join 2 A's together. Repeat 3 times, making 4 pairs. Press seam of each pair to one side.

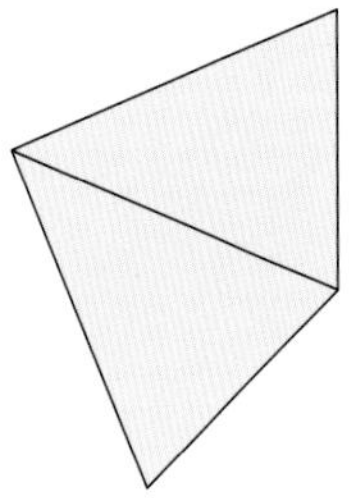

Paired A units

2 Join 2 A units to make half blocks. Repeat with other units. Press seams in a consistent direction.

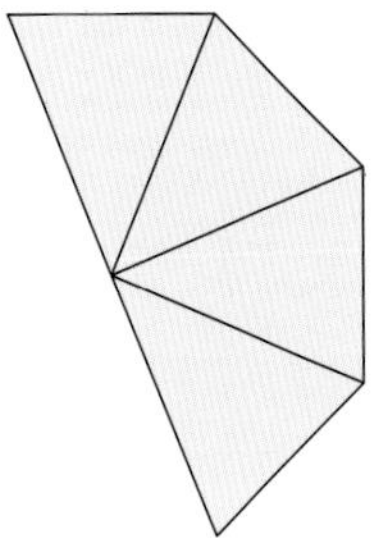

Half-block units

3 Pin half blocks together, matching points in the center of the block.

Tip: To match center points, place one pin exactly at the intersection of the seams; check front and back to make sure they are exactly aligned; add a stabilizer pin on either side of the middle pin.

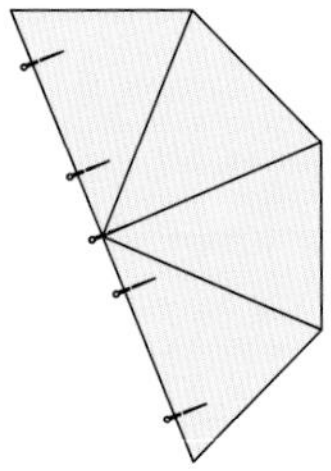

Half blocks pinned

4 Stitch half blocks together, and press seam.

Add the B corners to complete each block. Press each block. Check that the blocks measure 8¾" square. Trim if necessary.

Log Cabin blocks assembly

The Log Cabin blocks can be pieced in a variety of ways. For traditional piecing, follow the alphabetical order, adding strips one at a time in a clockwise direction, unless otherwise noted. Press seams toward the last strip added.

Quilt Top Assembly

1 Press each block. Lay the blocks out according to the Quilt Assembly Diagram.

2 Beach area: Sew pairs of rectangular Log Cabin blocks together to create squares when possible. Return them to the layout.

3 Sew the blocks in rows 1 and 2 together.

4 Sew the blocks in rows 3 and 4 together, checking the position of the umbrellas to insure that sea blocks are on top and beach blocks below.

5 Sew the blocks for rows 5 and 6 together, noting placement of the sailboat blocks and the square Log Cabin blocks at the ends of the rows and next to some of the sailboat blocks.

6 Sew the blocks in rows 7 and 8 together.

7 Sew the blocks in rows 9 and 10 together on each side of the sun.

8 Sew the blocks in row 11 together.

9 Sew the rows together to complete the quilt top.

10 Add the borders to the sides, then to the top and bottom of the quilt top.

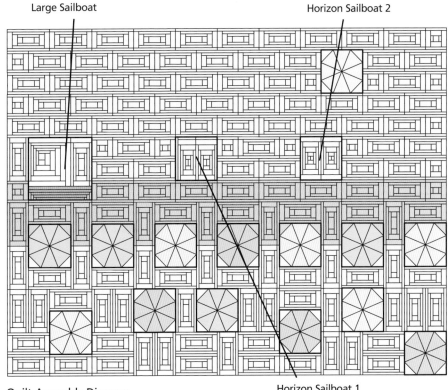

Large Sailboat

Horizon Sailboat 2

Horizon Sailboat 1

Quilt Assembly Diagram

FINISHING

See Quilting Basics, page 93, for general quilting and finishing instructions.

1 Layer the quilt top, batting, and backing; baste.

2 The umbrellas, sun, and sailboats were quilted near the seam lines to emphasize highlights and shadows. The sea was quilted in short repetitive waves; the sky has long rays quilted outward from the sun, across the sky. The border features a repetitive cresting wave motif.

3 Bind.

4 Attach a label and hanging sleeve.

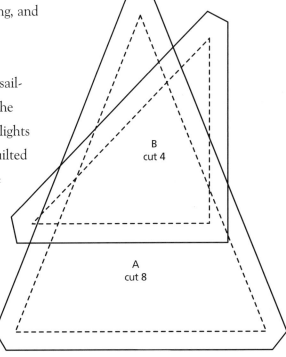

B
cut 4

A
cut 8

Patterns for Kaleidoscope block. Enlarge 110%.

fundy

Elsie Vrendenburg, Tustin, MI, 1997
Finished quilt size: 64½" X 52½"

The highlight of a delightful New England vacation was a trip to the Bay of Fundy. On the Canadian side we visited Mulholland and East Quoddy lighthouses; on the American side, we were enchanted by Whitlock's Mill and West Quoddy lighthouses, and the Lubec Channel Light. Part of the appeal of the lighthouses was the challenge of getting to them; East Quoddy, for example, can be approached on foot only at low tide, and the Bay of Fundy is famous for the speed of its incoming tide. Many people have been caught out in the middle of an empty bay by a wall of rushing water! Although this quilt looks very difficult to make, don't be daunted! If you work in sections, you will find that, though it is possibly not for beginners, this quilt is easier than it appears.

FABRIC REQUIREMENTS

Water print: ⅝ yard for outer border and Snail's Trail blocks

Red: 1¾ yard for inner border, optional piping, and details of lighthouses and sailboats

Blues: assorted dark, medium, and light fat quarters, fat eighths, and scraps to total 2½ yards for water and sky

White: one fat quarter for lighthouse bodies and seagulls

Black: 2 fat eighths, one of each, for lighthouse roofs, ledges, details on seagulls, rocks

Gray: assorted scraps for rocks, and a gray-and-white stripe for one lighthouse body

Red print: assorted scraps for boat sails, lighthouse trim, moss on rocks

Taupe/tan prints: assorted scraps for rocks

Greens: assorted fat quarters, fat eighths, and scraps for grass, trees, and meadows

Backing: 3¼ yards

Batting: 69" x 57"

Binding: ⅜ yard

Other supplies

Freezer paper

CUTTING

Water print: Cut borders and binding first and put them aside; use the remaining fabric for the Snail's Trail blocks.

From the lengthwise grain, cut 2 strips 4½" x 52½" for the side outer borders, then cut 2 strips 4½" x 56½" for the top and bottom outer borders.

Red: Cut 2 strips 1½" x 54½" for the top and bottom inner borders, then cut 2 strips 1½" x 44½" for side inner borders.

For optional piping, cut 2 strips ¾" x 52½" for the sides and 2 strips ¾" x 64½" for the top and bottom.

Binding: Cut 12 strips 2" x width of fabric.

Snail's Trail blocks

Refer to the quilt photo for color placement for each of the 36 blocks. For each block, you will need:

A: 4 squares 1⁹⁄₁₆" x 1⁹⁄₁₆".

B: 2 squares 2⅜" x 2⅜", then cut in half diagonally for 4 half-square triangles.

C: One square 3⅜" x 3⅜", then cut in half twice diagonally for 4 quarter-square triangles.

D: 2 squares 3⅞" x 3⅞", then cut in half diagonally for 4 half-square triangles.

BLOCK ASSEMBLY

Freezer-paper piecing

The construction technique for the lighthouse blocks is known as freezer-paper piecing. The freezer paper acts as individual single-use templates, which are ironed onto the fabric during construction, and later removed. You don't stitch through the paper, so it is easy to remove. It can be placed on the fabric exactly where you want it. The master copy remains intact for reference.

Note: If you prefer paper-foundation piecing, any subsections marked by broken lines may be foundation pieced. The pieces are sequentially numbered in piecing order, starting with the lowest number in the subsection. See page 95 for basic paper-piecing instructions.

1 Enlarge the patterns as specified on each pattern page. Be very careful to measure enlarged blocks before using them. Every copier is different, and the blocks must fit

together once constructed. The patterns are the reverse of the finished block, because you will be placing the templates on the wrong side of the fabric.

2 Tape freezer paper, shiny side down, over the master pattern. Using a ruler to keep lines straight, trace the entire pattern onto the dull side of the freezer paper. (The pattern is designed so you will not piece curves or set-ins, only straight lines.) Transfer all numbers to the freezer paper copy.

Note: The numbers on the individual pieces refer to piecing order.

3 Cut the freezer paper pattern into individual pieces. A rotary cutter with an old blade will work.

Note: It is less confusing if you cut and sew one block or block section at a time. However, if you choose to cut the pattern apart all at once, put the pieces for each section in separate, labeled envelopes until you are ready to use them.

Tip: Keep the original pattern handy, because you will need to refer to it frequently as you piece the block.

4 With a dry iron set on "cotton," iron the freezer-paper templates to the *wrong side* of the fabrics. Allow at least ½" between shapes.

You can eyeball the seam allowances, or place your ruler on top of the paper template, lining up the ¼" mark with the edge of the paper, so the ruler extends ¼" beyond the paper. Rotary cut along the edge of the ruler. Add a seam allowance to each side of all shapes.

Tip: As you cut each piece, place them paper side up on the corresponding section of the master pattern. This will help you put the "puzzle" back together, and you will know if you've missed any pieces.

5 Work on one section at a time. Sew the pieces together in the order in which they are numbered, beginning with the lowest number. Place the fabric shapes right sides together, and match up the corners of the freezer paper. If pinning is necessary, pin only in the seam allowances.

6 Stitch as close as you can along the edge of the freezer paper, without sewing through the paper.

7 Press each seam as you stitch, pressing toward the feature that appears to be in the front of the design whenever possible. (For example, you would press toward a building rather than toward the sky.) In areas where many seams come together, press some seams

open, to reduce bulk. On very small pieces, it helps to trim seam allowances to ⅛" to reduce bulk.

You can remove the paper from each piece after it has been sewn— on all sides—to other pieces.

Note: A few of the pieces in this design are very small, and the paper pieces can easily become buried underneath seam allowances. You can remove the tiny papers as you stitch these pieces to a larger one.

8 As each portion of a section is completed, lay it paper side up, on top of the master pattern. When you have all the parts of a major section completed, sew them together. Remove all paper, and lightly steam-press the section. Trim the edges to square up the block if necessary.

Snail's Trail blocks

Finished block size: 6" x 6"

Refer to the quilt photo for color placement in individual blocks. You may wish to create these blocks after the larger lighthouse blocks in order to match specific sections. You will need a total of 36 blocks (including 2 for the West Quoddy Light block, page 86).

If you use the same fabric in each quadrant or "arm" of the block, you will get more of a spinning effect. Also, you may substitute a seagull block for a center four-patch in any

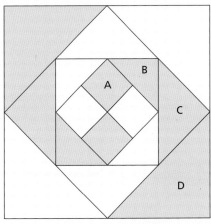

Snail's Trail block. Enlarge 267%.

Snail's Trail

Boat

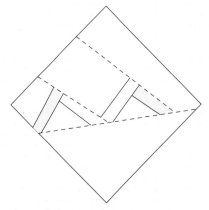

Seagull block. Enlarge 145%.

Snail's Trail block.

1 Sew 4 A squares (or a seagull block) together and press.

2 Sew B triangles to opposite sides.

3 Sew B triangles to the 2 remaining sides.

4 Repeat steps 2 and 3 with C triangles.

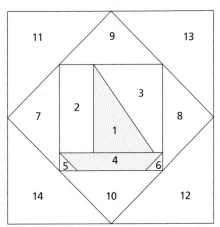

Boat block. Enlarge 267%.

5 Repeat steps 2 and 3 with D triangles

Boat block

Finished block size: 6" x 6"

Refer to the photo for color placement in individual blocks. You will need 2.

If you like, a boat block can replace any Snail's Trail block since they are the same size.

Sew the pieces together in the order in which they are numbered, beginning with the lowest number.

Whitlock's Mill Light block

Finished block size: 6" x 12"

Refer to the photo for color placement.

Details: Section 2, piece 9 is a window; piece 13 is railing—try a small black check or stripe

1 Cut apart the individual sections.

2 In each section, sew the pieces together in the order in which they are numbered, beginning with the lowest number.

3 Sew the sections together.

4 If necessary, trim to size.

Whitlock's Mill

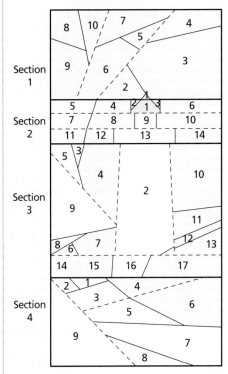

Whitlock's Mill Light block. Enlarge 320%.

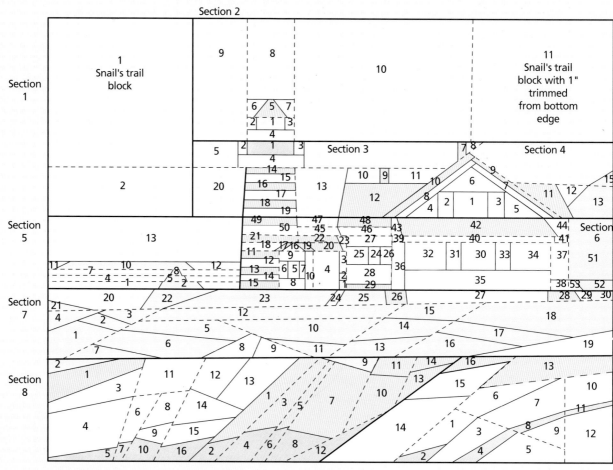

West Quoddy Light block. Enlarge 390%.

West Quoddy Light block

Finished block size: 24" x 18"

Refer to the photo for color placement. You will need 2 of the Snail Trail blocks, page 85, to complete this section.

Details:

Section 2, piece 1 is a window; piece 4 is railing—try a small black check or stripe.

Section 3, piece 4 is also railing.

Section 4, pieces 2 and 3 are windows.

Section 6, piece 5 is a window.

Section 7, pieces 26 and 28 are steps—try a small dark stripe.

1 Cut apart the individual sections.

2 In each section, sew the pieces together in the order in which they are numbered, beginning with the lowest number.

3 Sew the sections together.

4 If necessary, trim to size.

West Quoddy Light

East Quoddy Light block

Finished block size: 18" x 18"

Refer to the photo for color placement.

Details: Section 4, pieces 7 and 8 are windows.

1 Cut apart the individual sections.

2 In each section, sew the pieces together in the order in which they are numbered, beginning with the lowest number.

3 Sew the sections together.

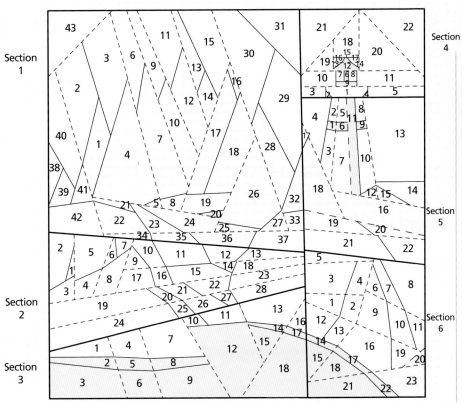

East Quoddy Light block. Enlarge 440%.

East Quoddy Light   Mullholland Light

1 Cut apart the individual sections.

2 In each section, sew the pieces together in the order in which they are numbered, beginning with the lowest number.

3 Sew the sections together.

4 If necessary, trim to size.

Lubec Channel Light block

Finished block size: 6" x 12"

Refer to the photo for color placement.

Details: Section 1, piece 1 is the light; pieces 2 and 3 are windows; piece 4 is railing—try a small black check or stripe.

1 Cut apart the individual sections.

2 In each section, sew the pieces together in the order in which they are numbered, beginning with the lowest number.

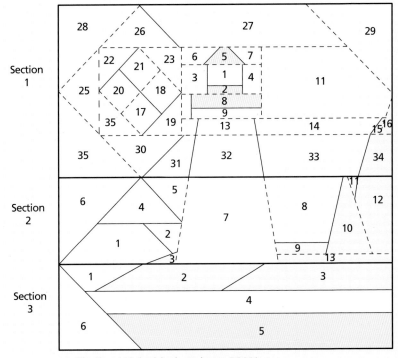

Mullholland Light block. Enlarge 330%.

4 If necessary, trim to size.

Mulholland Light block

Finished block size: 12" x 12"

Refer to the photo for color placement.

Details: Section 1, piece 1 is a window; piece 8 is railing—try a small red check or stripe.

3 Sew the sections together.

4 If necessary, trim to size.

QUILT TOP ASSEMBLY

1 Referring to the Quilt Assembly diagram, arrange blocks and light-house sections as shown, being careful to place Snail's Trail blocks in the right orientation to suggest ocean waves.

2 Stitch the blocks and sections together to complete the quilt top.

3 Trim to square up sides and corners.

Quilt Assembly Diagram

4 Add the top and bottom inner borders, then the side inner borders.

5 Add the top and bottom outer borders, then the side outer borders.

Note: Optional flat piping is added after the top has been quilted, before binding. See Finishing, Step 3.

FINISHING

See Quilting Basics, page 93, for general quilting and finishing instructions.

1 Layer the backing, batting, and quilt top. Baste.

2 Use free-motion stitching to outline all features and to add contour lines, waves, and other textures.

3 Flat piping (optional): for an extra special touch, add a little color just inside the binding with a flat piping. (See cutting directions) Fold piping strips in half lengthwise, wrong sides together. Press. Baste to the quilt top, with the raw edges of the piping even with the raw edge of the quilt, and with ends overlapped at corners.

4 Bind.

5 Attach a label and hanging sleeve.

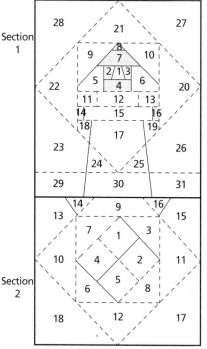

Lubec Channel Light block. Enlarge 330%.

Lubec Channel Light

Lights Along the Seaway Trail

44" x 34", Mary Knapp, Watertown, NY, 2001
Machine pieced and hand quilted. Photo by Jennie L. Cleary

Three Lighthouses

13" x 35", Mary Knapp, Watertown, NY, 2001
Machine pieced and hand quilted. Photo by Jennie L. Cleary

The inspiration for both *Lights Along the Seaway Trail* and *Three Lighthouses* were actual lighthouses and the feelings they evoke. The lighthouses are scattered along the Seaway Trail, which follows four major waterways in upstate New York and Pennsylvania. The choice of fabric and quilting stitches is meant to enhance the viewer's perception of Greek Revival, Stick, and Gothic styles as well as smooth and rough-cut limestone set in regular courses, domed cast-iron roofs, and windows that reflect the color of the hand-painted skies. I did this without adding clutter or "cute" to the lighthouses.

goldenrod
on the beach

Lita Star, Franklin Square, NY, 2001
Finished quilt size: 55" x 45"

This technique is spontaneous and template-free; the quilt is assembled and quilted simultaneously! Use this method to create your own special place in the sun.

Collect photographs of sunsets, water, and seashores for inspiration and color reference. Study the photos for colors that suggest how to shade the sand dune, for example, or how to make a splendid sunset.

FABRIC REQUIREMENTS

Muslin: 2 yards for foundation

Blues: assorted dark and light scraps (or fat eighths and fat quarters) for water, sky, and inner borders

Reds, pinks, and peaches: assorted scraps or fat eighths for sky

Gold and yellow: assorted scraps or fat eighths for sky, goldenrods, and details of sand dune

Creams, beiges, tans, browns, and grays: assorted dark and light scraps or fat quarters or fat eighths for sand and inside border

Dark brown/dark gray: assorted scraps for fencing, rocks, and shadows

Backing: 2 yards

Batting: 57" x 47"

Binding: ½ yard

Other supplies

Mechanical or other hard-lead pencil

Lightweight fusible web

Embroidery thread (hand or machine): green, yellow, brown, and gold

Threads to match fabrics

Decorative-edge scissors

Fabric spray adhesive

Fabric glue

Optional: Netting, tulle, or paint in gray, brown, gold/yellow for shadows

CUTTING

Muslin: Cut one strip 57" x width of fabric and 2 strips 7" x width of fabric.

Sky, water, sand, and dunes will be free-hand cut during the assembly of the quilt.

Binding: Cut 6 strips 2" x width of fabric.

QUILT TOP ASSEMBLY

1 Sew the 7" strips together at the short end. Press seam open. Sew to long side of the 57" foundation strip. Press seam open. Trim to 57" x 47". Lightly sketch the horizon line, an outline for the dunes, and the shoreline on the muslin foundation.

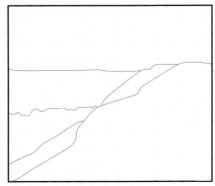

Sketch sections

2 Smooth the batting onto the wrong side of the backing; top with muslin.

3 Use fabric spray adhesive or pins to baste the layers together.

4 Select a background fabric that reminds you of sky; trim to fit and pin in place. Free-hand cut strips of sunset colors (you can use decorative cutters), varying the length, width, and color of the strips according to the photo. Pin the strips in place.

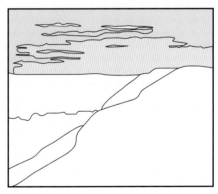

Arrange sky

5 Choose a background color for the water. Trim to fit and pin in place, then free-hand cut strips to add detail and depth.

Note: Overlap the sky at the horizon about ¼". Be sure to use lighter colors toward the horizon.

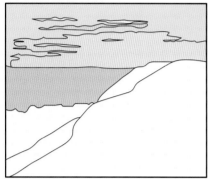
Arrange water.

6 Trim fabric for dune and shoreline, overlapping the water fabric ¼". Pin in place.

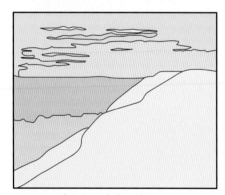
Arrange dune and shoreline.

7 Use a wide zigzag or long, straight stitch to sew all the pinned sky, water, and sand fabrics in place.

8 Following the manufacturer's instructions, fuse the fabrics you selected for rocks and fencing with a lightweight fusible web before cutting out shapes. Freehand cut shapes as desired.

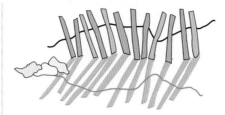
Couching

French knots

Tip: To add an illusion of depth, make elements such as fencing slats or rocks progressively smaller as they recede from the foreground.

9 Fuse, pin, or glue fencing and rocks in place as desired on the sand dunes. Free-motion zigzag or embroider around the edges of all shapes.

10 Hand- or machine-embroider goldenrods and other grasses and weeds. French knots are a good choice for the grasses. Couch embroidery floss along the top portion of the fence slats to suggest wire.

11 Add shadows as needed to complete the effect, using netting, tulle, or paint.

12 Highlight the water with embroidery or paint.

13 Trim the quilt top to finished size.

FINISHING

See Quilting Basics, page 93, for general quilting and finishing instructions.

1 Bind.

2 Add a hanging sleeve and label.

Fabric requirements are based on a 42"-width; many fabrics shrink when washed, and widths vary by manufacturer. In cutting instructions, strips are cut on the crosswise grain unless otherwise noted. A fat quarter is 18" x 22". A fat eighth is 9" x 22".

GENERAL GUIDELINES

Seam allowances. A ¼" seam allowance is used for most projects. It's a good idea to do a test seam before you begin sewing to check that your ¼" is accurate.

Pressing. In general, press seams toward the darker fabric. Press lightly in an up-and-down motion. Avoid using a very hot iron or over-ironing, which can distort shapes and blocks.

Borders. When borders strips are to be cut on the crosswise grain, diagonally piece the strips together to achieve the needed lengths.

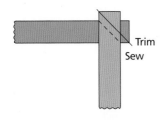

Trim
Sew

Butted Borders. In most cases the side borders are sewn on first. When you have finished the quilt top, measure it through the center verti-

cally. This will be the length to cut the side borders. Place pins at the centers of all four sides of the quilt top, as well as in the center of each side border strip. Pin the side borders to the quilt top first, matching the center pins. Using a ¼" seam allowance, sew the borders to the quilt top and press.

Measure horizontally across the center of the quilt top, including the side borders. This will be the length to cut the top and bottom borders. Repeat, pinning, sewing, and pressing.

Backing

Plan on making the backing a minimum of 2" larger than the quilt top on all sides. Prewash the fabric, and trim the selvages before you piece.

To economize, you can piece the back from any leftover fabrics or blocks in your collection.

Batting

The type of batting to use is a personal decision; if you aren't sure what type to use, consult your local quilt shop. Cut batting approximately 2" larger on all sides than your quilt top.

Layering

Spread the backing wrong side up and tape the edges down with mask-

ing tape. (If you are working on carpet you can use T-pins to secure the backing to the carpet.) Center the batting on top, smoothing out any folds. Place the quilt top right side up on top of the batting and backing, making sure it is centered.

Basting

If you plan to machine quilt, pin baste the quilt layers together with safety pins placed a minimum of 3"–4" apart. Begin basting in the center and move toward the edges first in vertical, then horizontal, rows.

If you plan to hand quilt, baste the layers together with thread using a long needle and light-colored thread. Knot one end of the thread. Using stitches approximately the length of the needle, begin in the center and move out toward the edges.

Quilting

Quilting, whether by hand or machine, enhances the pieced or appliqué design of the quilt. You may choose to quilt in-the-ditch, echo the pieced or appliquéd motifs, use patterns from quilting design books and stencils, or do your own free-motion quilting. Suggested quilting patterns are included in some of the projects.

Binding

Double-Fold Straight Grain Binding (French Fold)

Trim excess batting and backing from the quilt. If you want a ¼" finished binding, cut the strips 2" wide and piece together with a diagonal seam to make a continuous binding strip.

Press the seams open, then press the entire strip in half lengthwise with wrong sides together. With raw edges even, pin the binding to the edge of the quilt a few inches away from the corner, and leave the first few inches of the binding unattached. Start sewing, using a ¼" seam allowance.

Stop ¼" away from the first corner, backstitch one stitch. Lift the presser foot and needle. Rotate the quilt one-quarter turn. Fold the binding at a right angle so it extends straight above the quilt. Then bring the

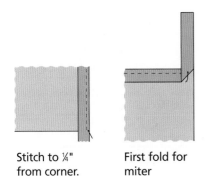

Stitch to ¼" from corner. First fold for miter

Second fold alignment. Repeat in the same manner at all corners.

binding strip down even with the edge of the quilt. Begin sewing at the folded edge.

Continuous Bias Binding

A continuous bias involves using the same square sliced in half diagonally, but sewing the triangles together so you continuously cut the marked strips. The same instructions can be used to cut bias for piping. Cut the fabric for the bias binding or piping so it is a square. If yardage is ½ yard, cut an 18" square. Cut the square in half diagonally, creating two triangles.

Sew these triangles together as shown, using a ¼" seam allowance. Press the seam open.

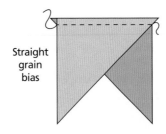

Straight grain bias

Using a ruler, mark the parallelogram with lines spaced the width you need to cut your bias. Cut along the first line about 5".

Join Side 1 and Side 2 to form a tube. Line A will line up with the raw

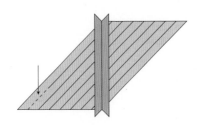

edge at B. This will allow the first line to be offset by one stripwidth.) Pin the raw ends together, making sure that the lines match. Sew with a ¼" seam allowance. Press seams open.

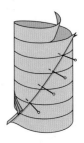

Finishing the Binding

This is one method of finishing the binding. Fold under the beginning end of the binding strip ¼". Lay the ending binding strip over the beginning folded end. Continue stitching beyond the folded edge. Trim the excess binding. Fold the binding over the raw edges to the quilt back and hand stitch, mitering the corners.

MACHINE APPLIQUÉ USING FUSIBLE ADHESIVE

Lay the fusible web sheet paper-side up on the pattern and trace with a pencil. Trace detail lines with a permanent marker for ease in transferring to the fabric.

Use paper-cutting scissors to roughly cut out the pieces. Leave at least a ¼" border.

Following manufacturer's instructions, fuse the web patterns to the wrong side of the appliqué fabric. It helps to use an appliqué-pressing